THE LITERATURE OF DEATH AND DYING

Experiences
Facing Death

BY

MARY AUSTIN

ARNO PRESS

A New York Times Company

New York / 1977

Reprint Edition 1977 by Arno Press Inc.

Copyright 1931 by The Bobbs-Merrill Company

Reprinted by permission of
The Bobbs-Merrill Company, Inc.

Reprinted from a copy in
The University of Illinois Library

THE LITERATURE OF DEATH AND DYING
ISBN for complete set: 0-405-09550-3
See last pages of this volume for titles.

Manufactured in the United States of America

Library of Congress Cataloging in Publication Data

Austin, Mary Hunter, 1868-1934.
    Experiences facing death.

    (The Literature of death and dying)
    Reprint of the ed. published by Bobbs-Merrill,
Indianapolis.
    1. Death. I. Title. II. Series.
BT825.A8 1977   128'.5   76-19557
ISBN 0-405-09553-8

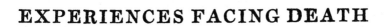

EXPERIENCES FACING DEATH

By MARY AUSTIN

Experiences
Facing Death

BY

MARY AUSTIN

Indianapolis
THE BOBBS-MERRILL COMPANY
Publishers

For
My Beloved Query
Who Will Understand
All That The Writer Has Failed To Say

FOREWORD

ON THE MEANING OF EXPERIENCE

NOBODY understands better than the author of this book that the title itself raises in important quarters, a question that invalidates the work as a whole. It raises the question as to what sort of occurrences may be properly included in the term experience. Because one can not read much beyond the first paragraph without realizing that what is described is so personal to the author, even when the reference is to phenomena that are conceded to have wide human occurrence, so individual in quality that it must inevitably lack the one characteristic which brings it within the domain preempted by science, the characteristic of measurability.

That none of it is beyond the range of intelligent and scholarly discussion, does not help much with an American public in whom intelligence is timorous and scholarship conventional. Especially as it is freely admitted by the author to be beyond the reach of such checks and standards as have been devised so far by apostles of what is known as the scientific method. It can not be put into a test tube or a crucible, can not be scaled up or down an array of instruments generally accessible, can not be so posed before an audience as to yield from the common factors of a generalized reaction, a stable unit of measurement. And by our accepted reading of the term, for all except the greatest scientists, the whole matter under discussion will be classed as inexperienceable.

For the type of mind that has accepted measurability as the one quality establishing the validity of experience, admitting the occurrence as to the standing of experience, as such, the whole range of subjects herein discussed, will be automatically relegated to the category of the delusive, the hallucinatory, the pathological, the abnormal. Not experiences themselves, but phantasmagoria of experience. That many readers will feel disposed to drop the book immediately on coming upon aspects of the subject-matter, which by their patent advertisement of immeasurability place themselves outside of the field of legitimately named experience, is a hazard the author has taken well into account. To those to whom a human happening is not truly "experience" unless it can be put through the laboratory, the averted mind's eye must be its own excuse. The especial handicap of the laboratory method is that it can deal successfully only with those occurrences which can, by taking thought, be *made* to happen. There are not lacking intelligences of the first order willing to admit types of human occurrences which, if they can not be tried out by laboratory appliances, can, nevertheless, be put through the personal instrumentation of other humans, from whom one may collect an infinite succession of angles of view, by means of which the whole compass of experience may be boxed, so to speak, and presumptive evidence of the reality at the heart of it arrived at. It is by this method that anything approaching a science of psychology or sociology can be reasonably postulated.

But even by this method we are constrained

to the study of occurrences whose point of origin can be reasonably conditioned. We would still be obliged to exclude from the category of experience all such interior adventures as occur of themselves. The whole race of Prophets and such prophetic starts and flashes as are known to occur even to the least distinguished individuals, would remain a total loss. We would be, by such a limitation of the term "experience" in exactly the situation of the mathematician who would admit the greatest common factor of a series of numbers and deny their least common denominator. In this situation, it is not surprising that certain superior minds have held out against the restriction of the term, experience, to happenings which can be made to recur at will by the investigator, and are disposed to include in it anything that has, for the individual, the quality of experience.

A very little consideration enables us to arrive at the conviction of alterations set up in the psyche, as the universal concomitant of what we designate as experience; however slight the change we know that we are never the same again. Experience does something to us. Conversely, whatever produces an alteration, a start, a motion of the psyche, is experience. This is the only resort Science can have against the puerility of admitting to the category of human occurrences only those which are objectively measurable. As a matter of fact, if our method were sufficiently delicate and extended, it is probable that all experience could be measured, even that of the appreciable presence of your long dead friend in the middle of the night, the appearance of a blue spark as a refuge from pain, as herein described, the convincing sensation many people confess to, of being temporarily out of the body's envelope.

It is with this understanding of the quality of experience as the determinant of change, especially in view of the professional importance of the wide angle of change that can be brought about in the work of a creative artist by a matter so slight as the way a shadow falls or the rhythmic value of a word, that the present work has been undertaken. Everything that can take place within the human psyche is admitted to the discussion. The point of the discussion being not the fact of the experience occurring as reported, but the extent to which any given experience can be assured to be what it reports itself as seeming to the recipient. It is probable that it is the convincingness of any occurrence *as experience,* and not a will to delusion which leads to its being stated positively in the terms in which it presents itself. A man does not say, I had an experience last night, I have no idea what it meant, or what was its origin, but it affected me as though my dead mother were in the room with me. What he says is, I felt my mother here in the room with me last night, and you are to understand by this that something happened to him, had an effect upon him, altered his attitude toward all experiences of that character in other men.

Singularly no one seems to have commented upon the extent to which man is dependent upon experiences describable only as experience, for his understanding of much that otherwise escapes his intelligence. Odd, he says, about this time-space business—I don't know

how they figure it out, but I've always had a
sort of feeling it must be that way. Or, I
know there is another dimension than this—
I've been there. You can be surer of a man
to whom these things have presented themselves as experience, than of the one who says
he believes these things because he has read
them in the book of Einstein, or the Koran,
or the Book of Mormon. Not that what is
in books is necessarily illusory, unsound or
deliberately falsified. But it can be in all
the books in the world and not be yours until
it has been experienced, until it has been taken
into the deep-self and originated an activity
there. It is the greatest of our educational
fallacies to suppose that because we have read
all the books, or even memorized them, that we
are therefore enlarged in our experience. Until you begin to try them out experimentally
the *Book of the Dead* and the *Bardo Thödol*
are mere intellectual curiosities.

That is how it was with me, when I lay
uncertain of recovery, and reviewed in my
mind all the world's lore of death, all the great
teachings about it. I reexperienced them in

the light of the experience which gave rise to them; I relieved the immemorial motions of man's mind in working out a technique of death that satisfied his experience. That is why one names such a re-collection of man's knowledge-ability of death, *Experiences* . . . because one is changed by it . . . because it gives rise to fresh surmises, new approaches.

There is no other determinant of values in reference to the experiences that arise unpremeditatedly in the deep-self. The explanations of such experiences have nothing to do with it. The worst thing that can happen to us at this stage is to suppose that they have. Deep within life, is the need to orient itself toward death; if it can only accomplish that orientation by hallucination, by delusive presentiments of dead friends, nevertheless it will be accomplished. What is of primary significance is that the thing occurs as experience, it is not written on tables of stone nor pronounced from on High; it takes place. The one incontrovertible item of our knowledge about death is that it gives notice of itself as motion, we go toward it, we go through it.

It never, to the last wave of a hand over the hill, loses its *goingness,* the unimpugnable quality of experience.

What I have tried to study in this book, is the movement of experience as we go toward death. Not the interpretation of experience as meaning this or that, as proving anything at all, but the thing going on in us, the movement of waters against an unknown shore, revealing its steeps and shallows, its penetrability.

M. A.

EXPERIENCES FACING DEATH

EXPERIENCES FACING DEATH

I

OF DEATH, man comes into the world knowing nothing and feeling universally that somehow he himself will never suffer it. Realizing
its inevitability he invents a myth to account
for his personal exemption; and later, as he
sees his contemporaries falling before him into
the general human certainty, he experiences a
secret pang of triumph, as though by some essential superiority he had been elected to survive. Finally, when the end leaps out at him
starkly, not to be evaded nor denied, the stout-
est fronts it with sudden consternation. That
was how it was with me, when, after a life
span which made death, though unwelcome, appear reasonable, I faced that possibility with
what was for me the nearest approach to fear
that I had ever known. And of all that I had
thought or observed about death, the last thing
I had expected was to be afraid of it.

Once before, in my early thirties, I was positively told that all I had to look forward to was the inevitable end of a dated period of disease; and my curiosity was, on the whole, disappointed when the event dwindled into the insignificance of a mistaken diagnosis. At that time, however, I was apparently well and unshaken by anything more annoying than a faint insistent pain. In the later instance, I could partly account for the unanticipated spasm of fear by crediting it to my being at the lowest ebb of a long and tormenting illness. Even when I was most securely confident of survival, I had never been sure that the change called "death" might not prove an ordeal. But at this particular time my disturbed state of mind sprang in some measure from the temporarily involved condition of the pledges and responsibilities of my life; for as soon as I had made some practical disposition of my affairs, I found the sense of excited apprehension abating. After that I had time to gather up my fear and question it in the face of my still undaunted conviction that human consciousness survives the dissolution of the body.

To my relief, I discovered that the structure

of a rational belief in survival—built up largely by analogies and inferences as most of our science is, though you will not always find scientists admitting it—remained intact. With death staring me in the face, my reasons for believing that there is no such thing, remained unaltered.

When I analyzed my state of mind, I recognized several separate urges leading me to deny death. One was an unwillingness to leave a world so abounding in beauty that I could frame no image of any other in which I would prefer to live. Another was the impetus to survive, the will to prolong the life processes I had begun. But more than these, there remained at the bottom of my consciousness a something which was profoundly unaware of any ground for supposing that life did not go on and on, untouchably, beyond both hope and fear. The thing that made me afraid had nothing to do with any abstract doctrine of immortality; it was something much more personal— something to do with my individual share in it.

There is no more reason to assume that every individual consciousness achieves a competent survival than that every conception arrives at conscious life. All adventures of change appear to be conditioned by what is going on around them; and if we admit logic to the adventure, it would be entirely reasonable to suppose that the change called death might be so conditioned as to make survival undesirable. In saying this, I must hasten to explain that I had never been afraid of any traditional peril that had been postulated for an after-life; nor had death ever presented itself to me as the final adventure of the spirit. As a matter of fact, most of my life had been spent in the kind of pursuits which, so far as our best information goes, offers the best chance of survival. If anybody gets past death, my chance seemed as good as the next one's.

The orthodox moralist, upon learning that as I faced the probable end I found myself repenting of nothing, would no doubt think my confidence exaggerated. By repentance I mean that intuitive judgment on our own lives which advises us that somewhere a wrong turn has been taken—a turn at which secondary impulses have prevailed against the fundamental

individual drive. It has always interested me
to know that the word Jesus used, ordinarily
translated "repent," means literally "turn
around and go back and begin again."

In the intervals of pain and sick-bed exigencies, I never felt the least necessity to live any
of my life over *differently*. I found myself regretting occasions when I had not been kind—
regretting that I had ever been unkind at
all. But in respect to those things which my
admirers—if I had any—would probably wish
to forget, curiously enough, I sighed a little
because there had not been more. I regretted
the narrow and repressive moralities in which
I had been brought up, if these had been in any
way responsible for my having lived less in-
tensively than I might—if these had made me
love or hate less, or less variously, than opportunity afforded. No, I did not regret my
hates—I have always hated lying and coward-
ice, and latterly I have spent a great deal of
energy hating war; nor did I regret any of the
emotions and actions that might have come under the ban of the morality to which I was born.
My sins, however, did not include any of the

more drastic offenses. I had never deprived anybody of life, nor cheated anybody of spiritual opportunity, nor represented truth otherwise than as it came to me—all of which would, I think, be meet for repentance. What I am trying to convey is that it was not any belated moral queasiness, nor any spiritual unease, which accounted for my surprising consternation in the face of possible dissolution.

I have called this fear surprising, because, as I have already said, faith and intelligence were still making the habitual response. But there it was, discount it however much you will by the simple fact that I was emotionally reluctant to leave a world which, at its worst, has always interested me tremendously. I have had—thank God!—some pretty bad times in this world; but still, of late, I have taken to being rather silent on the worldly things I have liked the most. It seems scarcely decent in the face of Messrs. Joyce, Mencken and the psychoanalysts, to insist that one goes about the world with a singing bird inside and a leaping flame on either hand. But it is permissible to say that I like my friends, my work, and my house here on the loma; and the thought that I should never again see the wild plum blossoms storm the banks of Peña Blanca, never hear the drums of the Keres calling up the He-rain with its wing hollows filled with evening blueness, smote me with an insupportable pang. I feel quite certain that, had I been forced to abandon this present level of consciousness at that moment, I should have haunted, not my house, but the familiar scene—morning headlands, the three Wind Rivers and the winding trails; I should have come back to the sound of the drums and the smell of the orchards. For one to whom beauty—the reality of natural things—had been the most spiritualizing influence in life, it was necessary to get back of the dread of separation from these things and trace the fear to its source; to recover a little from the suspicion that leaving this life would be more than could be supported with fortitude.

To make that clear, to describe how it was that I was not terrified at the idea of leaving life, but only of leaving *this* life, I shall have to go back to the very beginning of my thinking about these things and retrace the steps by which I built up my still unshaken conviction that personal consciousness persists beyond death. For what had upset me was not the doubt of continuity, but the fear of continuing to live in a state in which I could not avail myself of my principal means of spiritual sustenance and most of my enjoyment.

Unless I am to speak entirely in terms of theories and analogies—which would not be particularly profitable to me nor to the reader—I shall have to go back to the most personal of spiritual experiences: the experience of the Presence of God.

If I use that term, it must be understood that to me God *is* the experienceable quality in the universe. He is the Universal Consciousness out of which my own consciousness stems—never a person, only faintly descried in the inknowing core of perception as Being.

I must have been between five and six when this experience happened to me. It was a summer morning, and the child I was had walked down through the orchard alone and come out on the brow of a sloping hill where there were grass and a wind blowing and one tall tree reaching into infinite immensities of blueness. Quite suddenly, after a moment of quietness there, earth and sky and tree and wind-blown grass and the child in the midst of them came alive together with a pulsing light of consciousness. There was a wild foxglove at the child's feet and a bee dozing about it, and to this day I can recall the swift inclusive awareness of each for the whole—I in them and they in me and all of us enclosed in a warm lucent bubble of livingness. I remember the child looking everywhere for the source of this happy wonder, and at last she questioned— "God?"—because it was the only awesome word she knew. Deep inside, like the murmurous swinging of a bell, she heard the answer, "God, God . . ."

How long this ineffable moment lasted I never knew. It broke like a bubble at the sudden singing of a bird, and the wind blew and the world was the same as ever—only never *quite* the same. The experience so initiated has been the one abiding reality of my life, unalterable except in the abounding fullness and frequency of its occurrence. I can recall, even as a child, leaving the companions of my play to bask in it, as one might abandon the shade to walk in the sun. There is scarcely any time in my adult life in which it can not be summoned; with more effort at some times than at others. It is furthest from me when I am most absorbed in the emotional reactions of personal existence, but never entirely out of reach. Often it seems to float like a bubble beside me, and in moments of abstraction and relaxation, without my volition, it encloses me with ineffable warmth and light. It is on these occasions that I hear the Voice speaking a word or two that I need to know: "Wait," "Go Forward," "Trust this person or this occasion." It has the *feel* of a Presence, but it never manifests itself as a person. It comes nearest to that when it arrives in the midst of work, like a tall white Presence at my shoulder; but it never takes any personal shape, neither of ghost nor god nor angel. It is a force, a source of energy.

When I speak of warmth and light in this connection, these are analogies only. I see nothing with my eyes, feel nothing with my hands, hear nothing with my ears. Nor have I ever failed to know that the Voice is *inside* me, a portion of my innermost deep-self functioning; as much a part of my constitution as the clapper is of the bell. When this experience began to come, there were no such words as "subconscious" and "subliminal" in current use; but it was always clear to me that the sensation of light and warmth and the Voice were responses of my inner self to a stimulation whose source was beyond guessing. As soon as I began to hear of the autonomic nervous system, I recognized it as the seat of the responses by which the experience is conditioned. I am chary of using the term "subconscious" in this connection because I do not wish to confuse it with any of the operations of what we ordinarily call "mind" or "intelligence." As the brain is obviously not the seat of such experience, it can not be called mental. All that the intelligence can do is to account for and explain the experience.

It would be idle to pretend that in locating the response in the autonomic reflexes—in what my Indian friends later taught me to call the "Sacred Middle"—we have determined the absolute nature of the experience. For the space of this article I am satisfied—if the reader is—to call it "God," or the "Great Unconscious." And for reasons that will come later, I have so much more confidence in the revelations that come from this experience, that if my Sacred Middle tells me that life is ever-living and the human frame only one of its abiding places, I will believe it much sooner than I would believe my intelligence, or the intelligences of Bertrand Russell or Albert Einstein, who are the most quoted prophets of extinction.

Probably there is nothing in this experience of mine that is different, except in its explicitness and persistence, from the experience of my contemporaries. Most people probably go on all their lives trusting their intelligence or their traditions for the unimportant issues, and for vital matters listening to the voice of the Sacred Middle, which they explain according to the mythological beliefs in which they have been brought up.

II

I SHALL have to interrupt myself here, as many times in this narrative, to explain the particular meaning that attaches in my mind to the terms "myth" and "mythology." It may help us past many of the difficulties that arise out of our modern lack of any competent vocabulary in which to carry on such discussion. A myth is primarily an attempt to express the mysterious in terms of the familiar—thunder as the clapping wings of a great bird, sea-tides as the alternate gulping and spewing of a great beast; God as the Father. Probably all the terms of Being in which mankind has immemorially described his intimate experience, are pure myths, the truth that underlies such experience, still escaping all the words by which it is familiarly called. By this definition the term "God" is a myth, referring to the as yet indescribable source of religious feeling, and by no means to a bearded Jewish patriarch with tribal emotions and a marked inferiority complex. Nor do I, in characterizing as Christian mythology the vocabulary of the religiosity in which I was brought up, mean to minimize either the experience it embodied, nor to invalidate the faith on which it was erected.

If we are to talk together intelligently on this subject we must elucidate our vocabulary as we go along. I shall spare no pains to apprehend the reality behind your myth, and insist that you refrain from supposing that my own mythology, drawn as it is from further afield, lacks a compensating reality.

I would not have you, for instance, suppose that when I speak of my Sacred Middle, I am merely being picturesque. I mean that central complex of nerves, ganglia, viscera, which was once thought of as the factual seat and source of courage, compassion, love, anger and premonition. Only I think of it not as the source, but as the receiving center of promptings, pulsations, communications, if you will, from sources older, more experienced than the intelligence, therefore in many respects more trustworthy. It is only a minority, and that the most urban, of the Intelligentsia who suppose that the seats of reality are all located in a narrow strip above the eyebrow or in a more insistent region below the belt, and have forgotten or will not admit that they have any middles. They forget that life began with a middle and a skin and got on some eons with very little else, not thinking at all, and dividing its middle when it desired to reproduce. They forget that within the complex of vital organs served by the autonomic system, lies the complete cycle of life experience in body building, repair and renewal of parts. Here are stored all memories of the patterns and the motions life has made. Here are all possible tendencies and techniques, which, when filtered through the intelligence, become the source of invention and achievement. All that has happened to life is remembered here, lying latent against need, once we have learned the trick of recalling it to the level of conscious intelligence. Here also resides that curious living experience which certain types of men feel it their duty to deny, simply because it is no part of man's conscious equipment—the experience of faith.

By faith I mean neither intellectual belief

nor the blind forcing of allegiance to a tradition. I mean exactly what Paul of Tarsus meant— *the evidence of things not seen*, the evidence of life's capacity to triumph over objective difficulties by developing organs and functions not yet discovered by the scientist's microscope. I mean the knowledge-feeling which enabled primordial protozoa to climb up out of the sea border, to live on the land and sail through the air, creating the mechanism necessary to these changes out of *the substance of things hoped for*.

Something within all life knows all the ways possible to life. In the higher creatures this knowledge-feeling becomes more or less conscious. When it refers to the less important issues, men call it a "hunch" and often trust it against their intelligence. When it refers to matters of the scope of life-continuance, men have also trusted it for the most part, translating it into myths, objectifying it with rites and ceremonials. From time to time the knowledge-feeling of exceptional individuals has embodied itself in philosophies and dogmas, which, because they express a general wide-spread certainty, have had wide acceptance. Later, when the particular explanation has been superseded by larger certainties, there are always a great many people who suppose that because the explanation had been discovered to be inadequate, the embodied perception of reality had been completely disproved. Nothing could be more mistaken.

Faith—the witness of unaccomplished things, the worker in the substance of desire—in so far as it deals with immortality, has passed through all these phases many times. But for the writer, nothing so irrelevant to experience as the current explanations of the things going on inside man (most of which have changed several times in my lifetime), shakes the evidence of my Sacred Middle as to the existence of the thing itself. Shrinking as one's physical organism naturally and healthily does shrink before the near approach of dissolution, nothing anywhere in the Middle of me denied the existence of the undying spark. When I thought I was about to shuffle off this mortal coil, I was not daunted by the fear that the essential *I* wouldn't be there still, perfectly aware of myself, and with a recognizable budget of personal characteristics. The thing I feared was that I might go on living, stripped of most of the things that made going on interesting and worth while. Intellectually I was still convinced of survival—as I shall presently take time to explain—but my disturbed state of mind arose from the fact that this conviction had failed to provide me with any comforting notion of how life would go on, and under what conditions.

The Western World has so long rested under the Christian prepossession about the life to come, that it does not invariably throw off that prepossession along with the dogmas of which it was the outcome. The Christian idea has always been that death, if not the end of life adventure, is decisive, and that the remaining course is then marked out one way or the other, without appeal. The disembodied one continues much the same person, minus his most objectionable human traits, and lives much the same life, rid of its most troubling phenomena.

Even the less orthodox versions of life after death, do not seem to have improved greatly on the hymn-book heaven of the early Christian saints. I recall in particular a forecast of spirit life by that distinguished prophet of spiritism—Sir Arthur Conan Doyle—in which it appeared that spirits might still suffer the necessity of the daily shave; and, as Sir Arthur explained, since we could not imagine ourselves losing our natural modesty along with our mortal frames, we should still be subject to the tyranny of clothes. All of which seemed to me a bit sillier than the Methodist Heaven of uninterrupted harp-playing, in which belief I was brought up.

And yet, what *do* we know of the essentials of discarnate existence which justifies us in presuming anything more acceptable? What frightened me was the realization that the little we could assume with any degree of safety, sounded neither easy nor interesting.

The creative writer is beset by a mysterious compulsory honesty which impels him to create shapes of beauty, but prevents him from living in them comfortably, because that compulsion forces him to go on for ever uneasily testing out the underpinning of his ideals, squaring up their corner stones by standards of reality which a succeeding generation will discover to be untenable. Something of that mysterious and compulsory honesty led me to realize that I had been imagining a future life in which the conditions would be those which I most desired. I had imagined a future equally free of harp-playing and of writing on slates for greasy mediums at a dollar a slate, but one in which I should drift pleasantly about the beloved scene, rid of the necessity of going to bed at night and of coming in when it rains. What I wanted was uninterrupted eons in which to explore the beauty and mystery of nature; and for byplay, I had incorporated in my eternity an idea that Thomas Hardy imagined after he accepted Einstein's theory of time-space—namely, that the time-stream might actually spread out behind us, undiminished by a single instant, infinitely explorable once we have learned the trick.

There was an occupation to which an immortal might happily apply himself! Imagine going back and forth unhindered in the endless stream of time, visiting the spacious days of great Elizabeth, finding the great Achilles, whom we loved! Now suddenly, all this became as unsubstantial as a small child's dream of Christmas.

Like a Christian, I had been thinking of keeping all the mechanism of sensory perception, of seeing color and feeling form and hearing music, together with the pageant of nature and history. And the one thing we positively know about death is that it takes from us the mechanism of all sensory experience. But in my case the loss of sensory mechanism would leave me stripped of the occasions which afford that other experience already described, which, after reading Brother Lawrence, I should call "The Practise of the Presence of God."

There are times in the life of the individual, when one's whole ancestry, the strength and sense of the race, rises up to meet some swift personal emergency. It rose for me now when I found myself insistently demanding: *What*

am I and *what have I* with which to defend myself against the dissolution of my present frame
and habit of being, with which to resist the reabsorption of my identity into the stream of undifferentiated consciousness?

III

ALTHOUGH I did not realize it at the time, this visitation of fear, in the face of undiminished certainty, was the test of the reality of the experience of the Presence of God as a factor in my spiritual life. By all the traditions of my time and upbringing, I should have rejoiced in the dissolution of my bodily frame as securing for me, for the term of eternity, that spiritual rapport of which the experience described had been but a foretaste. And, immediately I found myself facing that eventuality, I saw that I was without any assurance that this was so. I had experienced God with my Middle, just as I had experienced Beauty, which is the sensuous aspect of God, with my ears and my eyes; and how was I to be sure of reexperiencing either of them, lacking the essential instrument? How was I to know that death of the instrument does not constitute a recession of the spirit; that in dying I should not be carried further from the God my Middle knew.

What I was really afraid of was not death

as extinction, but death as a future state in which I should find myself stripped of my dearest purchase of living.

I do not mean to present this view of it as a unique personal experience. As I was aware, from my studies in primitive lore, it is actually an ancient and widely disseminated fear of mankind. The clever Greeks had imagined a hereafter of drab limitations on no account to be preferred to the pains and anxieties of the flesh. The more practical-minded Egyptians spent themselves upon devices for avoiding a future so little to be desired, and in particular, for securing the inestimable privilege of "coming forth by day." Years ago, while at work on a life of Jesus* I had been struck by the exaggerated values attached to the story of his supposed resumption of the body after the presumption of his death by crucifixion. Actually, at that time, only one sect of the Jews officially rejected the doctrine of personal survival, although doubt of the future had crept into the minds of the intellectuals of all the then known civilizations.

*A Small Town Man. Mary Austin. Harper's.

In the light of my own experience, it grew upon me that the reassuring item of the resurrection story had been the reappearance *in the flesh,* capable of all the familiar habituated acts of the flesh, offering them in confirmation of identity. Belief in the resurrection of the body was incorporated in the Christian creed because there was fear in the ancient pagan heart of just what I feared at that moment, continued life of the spirit stripped of the spirit's accustomed instrument.

An experience correlated with the illness which brought on the crisis of that fear singularly pointed the occasion. Because of physical idiosyncrasies which make it inexpedient for me to avail myself of the usual anesthetics and anodynes for pain, I have several times been pushed to the farthest edge of self-help to escape its humiliations. Minor afflictions can be evaded, for it is no longer considered a symptom of incipient mental decay to admit that one does evade them, by pushing the responsibility far back into the region inadequately described as the subconscious.

Twice, by efforts of desperation, I had abandoned situations pronounced by the doctors—for one can not go back of what one is told in these cases—to be of the utmost seriousness. Once, in a single night, I had shed a train of physical disabilities accumulated through several years of natural misadventures and inadequate medical attention—shed them as a tree sheds its leaves, and possibly by an analogous process of a complete withdrawal of consciousness. Experimentally acquainted with the method familiar to almost every creative worker, of flooding a neglected area with healthy consciousness, "turning on the juice" in deliberate efforts of self-renewal, I was ready to accept the superiority of consciousness over its physical host. I was quite ready to accept even the possibility that consciousness might pass from one envelope to another.

Any one remotely acquainted with the phenomena of hypnotism, trance, and some forms of autosuggestion, will recall that, under those conditions, consciousness behaves as though it could abandon its physical host for periods occasionally prolonged into months, or that it can apparently retire completely from definite areas, or even appear to take up its residence in some object wholly outside the body. Medical science is making experimental use of these behaviors of consciousness to promote health and aid in the repair and renewal of tissues that have been rent by surgery.

The writer has never been clever at utilizing these widely admitted possibilities, partly because there has been little demand for it. But in this emergency, unable to make use of hypnotic drugs, I discovered by accident that the recurrent intervals of pain could be escaped by projecting my consciousness into a remote blue spark, where I tucked up my feet, so to speak, and waited for the occasion of pain to pass. The blue spark was not imagined; it was discovered when I was fleeing not so much from pain as from the terror of the drugs which would have stopped the bodily pain only to leave the abused consciousness wandering in a private hell of its own, more to be dreaded than any physical pang.

Once discovered, the spark was always available for relief; but if I put off jumping too long, hoping the pain would turn out a false alarm, or waiting to see what the nurse could do, I had to take several running jumps before I could make it. Once inside, however, I was safe *so long as I remained conscious of being there*. But if, through the natural physical relaxation of relief, I fell asleep, I woke up presently in the here and now, with its attendant agony. I learned by practise to secure a certain amount of rest by keeping, as it were, one eye open on the spark, blue and infinitely small and isolated. But if I failed to be to some extent constantly aware of it, I fell into my body again, and had to submit to the humiliation of dope.

After this experience, there began to creep upon me a question as to whether escape from the ills of bodily existence might not involve a similar return to an original state of nature. I began to realize that though there remained intact, as the very core of consciousness, the knowledge of Immaterial Reality, which for convenience we call God, all my ways to and from that certainty were along mechanisms which death would more than likely dissolve. I was appalled to realize the extent to which most of those appreciations of natural beauty which make up the greater part of my spiritual experience, came through the sensory apparatus, which often becomes inoperative during life.

And what warrant is there that conscious intelligence, which is a late outgrowth of the spirit, will not also disappear with the brain by which it is instrumented? It was then that I began to recall that the Greeks imaged the innumerable host of the dead as flitting through a gray world emptied both of desire and the creative will. When you think of how many of the living seem to go about in a similar state, this begins to appear as a reasonable inference. Taken in connection with the teaching of all the great prophets of survival, like Jesus, who taught that immortality is more or less contingent upon maintaining a certain spiritual awareness in this life (*Except ye abide in me . . . ye shall not see the Father*), my experience with the blue spark as the resort of relief began to seem also prophetic.

What I said to myself at this point was: Suppose my conviction of being somehow able to get through the narrow gate of death means no more than that I shall get through. Suppose that I find myself the day after death, stripped to the dimensions of a spark, a spark of consciousness completely incapacitated by the act of death from resuming the only medium of expression with which I am acquainted. Suppose this whole business of recreating a spiritual envelope is to do over again, a new medium to evolve, a new personality to build, a new birthright of expressiveness to buy back at an unreckoned cost.

Many prophets have so taught and disciples so believed. As a doctrine, I had never been in the least interested in reincarnation. I found myself now in the position of having to consider whether or not it might be one of those myths— like the myth of the Judgment—with which mankind has masked the face of undetermined reality. Suppose what I am confronted with is the choice between beginning again such another long fumbling struggle for an adequate expressiveness, such as death is supposed to close, and an undeterminate hereafter as a poor gibbering ghost? Gibbering!

This was with me a more than ordinarily poignant anticipation, since I have not only had to go through the usual struggle of a rational being for a reasonable frame of being, but at the same time I had been suffering the creative artist's anguished search for expressiveness. Nor was the situation alleviated by the weariness of age, which is said to reconcile one to the curtailment of activity. Although this envelope of personality which has been won, is less ample and resplendent than I would like to have it, it still keeps my Middle warm and insistent. I do not feel to myself in the least moth-eaten!

In this situation, then, what I wanted most was the resort of human experience. I wanted to exchange views and suppositions, to rid my fears by exposing them to speech and prop my doubts by the confidences of my friends. And the amazing, the appalling, discovery was that there was no such resort to be had.

IV

It seems important to the writer at this point, that the reader should realize that the gesture behind this statement is not of persuasion but confession. I am not trying to make a point in favor of individual survival. I am trying to describe, as far as possible in the very rhythm and pattern of the experience itself, how, checked at the high point of a career devoted largely to considerations other than personal, I was suddenly confronted with the necessity of proving out a conclusion about the nature of my essential self. And up to this time my experience of myself had been experimental and instinctive rather than rational. In the previous chapters I have attempted to suggest the type of experience upon which I had to fall back in an emergency for which the modern intellectual world provides neither remedy nor suggestion. Equally incapable of accepting a doctrine of extinction, or a contrary belief in the orthodox hereafter of any organized religion known to me, I was obliged to resort my convictions, both intellectual and emotional. In view of my major prepossession in favor of the immense importance, the probably ever-living quality, of human consciousness, and my major determination to live as long as possible in this present frame, I had to strike a new equilibrium.

And my first appalled discovery was of the dreadful paucity of counsel, of genuinely determinative aid to that end. I not only did not know where to read for help; I did not know anybody with whom I could satisfyingly talk, for I particularly wished not to talk with anybody who had *accepted* his conclusions, whether from a religious or secular source. What I wanted was to exchange wayfarer's news with any one who, like myself, was convinced of survival as an innate possibility, without being committed to any particular mode of accomplishing it. I wanted to know, for example, whether anybody besides myself felt as I did, that the individual himself has something to do with his own survival; or whether any one of a similar intellectual background felt convinced that death is something we have to accept, like birth, with perhaps no other privilege connected with the event than that of kicking and squalling when it happens to us.

The period covered by the life of the writer is precisely that one in which the greatest possible alterations have taken place in the proprieties of what may, and may not, be talked about. It goes back to the time when women in particular were too ignorant to talk intelligently about sex had they wished to, but so little wished it that even the obviously imminent arrival of the "little stranger" was not supposed to be referred to in general conversation until it had been announced on specially selected stationery appropriately tied with pink or blue ribbon. Having lived from the time when the mere existence of sexual desire was, for women, a whisper in the corner, to that of hearing young women publicly declare themselves suffering from sex starvation; having passed through the period in which dissent from Christian orthodoxy was a thing good breeding demanded should be kept to yourself, to the present reversal of both rules; I had rather taken it for granted that the changes in the way in which death and its attendant phenomena may be mentioned had followed the same pattern of expansion.

You may talk of dreams now, of telepathy and hunches and apparitions and ouija boards, in circles where once the mention of these things elicited either the drawn lip of moral disapprobation, or the barely repressed *bosh!* of the professional intellectual. But not having had occasion for a quarter of a century to discuss death personally, it came as a shock to me to discover that all the new approaches to the subject exhibited precisely those reactions which the present generation has been at most pains to inhibit in respect to birth and sexual life. When I undertook to discuss what was naturally and healthily occupying my mind, I found myself shushed and consoled, or reproved, or tactfully diverted, according to the temper of the company, exactly as it happened fifty years ago when I asked my elders things nice girls weren't supposed to know.

When I was young, and Christianity still the prevailing expression of spiritual conviction, death was treated with dignity, as the inevitable antechamber to the soul's great adventure. Warned of death's approach, it was conceded that one had dispositions to make, factual and spiritual readjustments. It was permitted to discuss such matters fully with one's family and friends. One's religious confrères offered counsel and comfort; there were rites, services of prayer and admonition which could be requisitioned. As a matter of fact, I discovered that by accepting postulates of the various organized religions in my neighborhood, I could have commanded their spiritual and ritualistic resources without difficulty. What I couldn't get at any available price, was the serious, intellectual, undoctrinate discussion of survival as a psychological possibility. Against every effort of mine to reorganize my own consciousness in view of that possibility, there arose around me a conspiracy of refusals, of horrific avoidance of the subject, not lacking in intimations of hysteria such as I recall surrounded the introduction into ordinary conversation forty years ago, of such topics as divorce or eugenics.

Later, when it appeared that the crisis of illness had passed, though how far from triumphantly only myself and my physician knew, an effort on my part to provide for the disposal of as much of my baggage of personality as seemed unlikely to be taken with me on the last adventure, revealed that—with the sole exception of a friend who happens also to be a poet—there were but two reactions to be countered. One was that my wish to dispose of my body intelligently was simply one of those "queer" and slightly unseemly performances to which genius is liable, and the other that it was a "morbid" hangover from the pathological conditioning of illness, which, if sternly repressed by my friends, would pass away with returning health. So far were all my friends from realizing that what was in my mind came there as the result of a decision intellectually arrived at, that in the end, I went off privately and made my arrangements with as much concern for keeping the public uninformed, as forty years ago I would have made for concealing an illicit love-affair. And for the same reason. Not because I would be ashamed of it, but because I discovered that I couldn't expect anybody to understand what I meant by it.

If we accept the conclusions of the new psychology that the conversational inhibitions of the Victorian era arose out of repressions and their resultant fears and morbidities, I do not see how we can fail to realize in our current attitudes toward so natural an adventure as death, a similar morbidity of fear. What else can we conclude when the world's most talked about scientist insists that only feeble-mindedness or "ridiculous egotism" can beget the idea of personal survival, and an editor of a magazine which braves the conventions of sex-mention to the point of legal liability, declares publicly that his notion of the good life involves the inhibition of any mention of death?* What one suspects here is the same note of hysteria which makes obscenity out of an editorial by H. L. Mencken or a novel of Theodore Dreiser's. How are we to attain to a healthful idea about life, when we cherish even in the very center of our intellectual and esthetic ex-

*Albert Einstein, of course, and George Jean Nathan of the *American Mercury.*

istence, a fear so little subject to intelligent discussion and an inhibition so childish about the inevitable end of life?

Courage is no longer a virtue; it is, we are given to understand, an arrangement of the glands which must be compensated for or evaded by individual intelligence. Americans in general, it seems, suffer a glandular resistance to the idea of death which makes them not only averse to talking about it, but anxious to evade its mention by every sort of diddling phraseology and the revolting manipulations of "morticians." It remains for us who are not afraid of being afraid, or have at least got out of the habit of accepting our fears as a bias of behavior, to make what we can of them as an aid to discovery. Few discount the percentage of fear which would naturally arise out of *any* sudden, irreparable sundering from friends, occupations and places we have loved, and try to see how the remainder can be made to serve, as fear so often has served, the uses of life.

I have confessed to being afraid when I hadn't expected to be. I was appalled at the lack of ready-to-use material for composing or allaying those fears; and I ended by being astonished at the support I was able to collect out of the material of my life, for a new fronting of death in which fear is reduced to the degree that any intelligent person may admit without loss of dignity. And in view of the prevailing fear which I seem to have uncovered on all sides, among people unable to avail themselves of the support of a codified religion, it seems worth while to try to account for the items which have enabled me to arrive at a less timorous attitude toward an eventuality which, at the best, can not be postponed for more than another score or so of years.

From this point on, this book will be concerned with the path traveled by my mind while I lay between intervals of pain—which acts always with me as an acute stimulus to intellectualization—watching the immediate horizon for the appearance of the unwelcome visitor. This is the path of a mind better furnished than most with the sort of information likely to be illuminative, the mind of a practised folklorist which is not altogether without the flare of divinations proper to a poet, above everything else unlikely to be deceived by its own motions, experienced as these are in the professional patterns of story-telling. But before going on to those turns of the path which seem most worth recalling, another divagation is necessary to explain why these things are not reported in the ritual of evidence, but rather in the rhythm of experience; why the writer must not be thought of at any point as "arguing with you, but just as telling you."

One of the absurdities of our complete surrender to the ritual of science, is the ease with which two scientific conclusions can be made to nullify each other by the simple expedient of shouting "the will to believe" or "the will to disbelieve." In this manner scientists, who fail to realize that what are known as logic and the scientific patter are little more than ritualizations of the male approach, are enabled to fall back comfortably on their prejudices in matters not subject to the laboratory method. By the perfection of this ritual man has forged so excellent a medium of communication from mind to mind that we have been persuaded to overlook its complete obfuscation of the natural processes of the mind itself. By means of this invention man has enabled himself to enjoy the completely inutile intoxication of discursive inquiry into how many angels can dance on the point of a needle, as well as to confirm himself in the conclusion that women, by their general refusal of the ritual, are self-convicted of an inferior mental status. I am entirely willing to admit that it has become the weakness of women to-day, as in the beginning of social evolution it was their essential strength, to fail of intellectual curiosity toward everything but the experienceable properties of the universe. But I am still far from admitting that the experienceable issues of life can be dealt with only, or properly at all, by the male ritual. I go so far, even, as to suspect that both science and politics lag in essential particulars because of our rather obstinate insistence on the sole male approach; that we might understand both the pattern of evolution and the pattern of the good life better if we conceded that they are better studied by the ritual of life processes, especially exemplified for us in what transpires within the female complex. Deep within the womb of life there may be activities going on, which have for their fruit the evolution of souls, and immortal existence. I am at least aware of processes going on within myself, which I nominate by that title. What I propose to myself is to report on the evidence of such processes as they make themselves felt at the intellectual level, much as the process of child-bearing gives notice of itself, capable of being reasonably considered.

If I have an ever-living soul, its ever-livingness must be discoverable in me as a child in the womb, and it is at such crises as I have described, when its ever-living properties are about to be tested out by the adventure of death, that they are most likely to give notice of themselves.

If, in my case, the phenomena which might be considered as arising out of an immortal quality in the psyche, are more evidential than is generally the case, it is possibly because I am by profession both poet and novelist as well as female. This means that I am naturally committed to those strongly directive reactions with which the heredity middle of mankind is always more or less endowed. Without this capacity for robustly visceral autonomic reactions, one can not become a novelist at all; one teaches school or runs a tea shop with antiques on the side, or becomes a lady realtor—employments for which a vital Middle is not a necessary accompaniment. By the daily business of making a living, a novelist necessarily brings into constant play the whole range of reactions which I have called feeling-knowledge. The first thing a creative writer learns, is to handle his feeling-knowledge sincerely and respectfully. That is what I mean by saying that I believe my Middle against my intelligence whenever I find them in conflict.

If, in this case, I found both my feeling-knowledge and my intellectual conclusions in tolerable accord, a contributory reason might be discovered in that aspect of my work which has for forty years brought me into close personal contact with primitive peoples. When not actually neighboring with Indians, I am reading about them, talking with other students of their lives and customs, fighting for them or explaining them to their benefit. Thus I have come intellectually to realize how utterly dependent man has been on his feeling-knowledge during that long period in which his intelligence has been evolving. It is only by reliance on vital reactions that man has saved himself alive during the minority of the intellect, which is almost always wrong except as it permits itself to be instructed by the deep-self. What I have come to realize is that science—the evolution of the intellectual approach to reality—is very largely a business of supplanting one intellectual error by another one. I am therefore prepared to discard all the intellectual conclusions either for or against survival, even those I invent myself, for the sake of holding on to my innate conviction that something in me does not die when I let go my hold on physical reality.

There is another aspect of the experiences which are here described, which grows out of the writer's business of creative writing. It will serve to explain why in the crisis of fear no effort was made to derive comfort from the attempts everywhere undertaken, to pierce the veil of oblivion by means of what goes by the name of Psychic Research.

The determining character of all such attempts is, that they depend upon a secondary approach by way of the levels which are generally conceded to lie below the threshold of intelligent self-consciousness. It makes no difference whether the evidential revelations come through the self of the seeker, or some other self, called a medium; they are always produced out of the region from which the novelist daily and hourly draws the matter and the form of his product. Even when the mediumistic phenomena are objective, as in table-tipping or tambourine-playing, they are assumed to be of subjective origin.

To take the measure of his own subconscious capacity, to control and direct it, to take advantage of its sudden spurts of superiority and restrict its lapses into infantilism, is the first business of the practising novelist. It becomes— the deep-self of the creative writer—another entity almost, with which he learns to live and never to be surprised at, an entity knowing so much more than his immediate sensory self, that it should never really surprise him to discover that it knows what becomes of the dead. Many novelists do actually accept mediumistic phenomena as evidential. Others discover the capacity of this subliminal self for something that I have called elsewhere,* sleight of mind, since psychologists have so far failed to name it. It is so quick, this other entity—as much quicker than the intellect as the cat is quicker than the mouse—so inherently anxious to arrive at the given point before the intelligence can forestall it, that it performs tricks equivalent to sleight of hand, tricks that occasionally deceive its host. Watching this performance in the less pretentious and often more pellucid mind of tribal man, and in other animals, it seems to me that sleight of mind is perhaps related to protective mimicry and deserving of the same discriminating study. It is, at any rate, just this experiential knowledge of delusive tricks of the subconscious, that keeps the present novelist from taking the mediumistic evidences of survival too seriously. Of recent developments of mediumistic phenomena, such

*Everyman's Genius. Mary Austin. Bobbs-Merrill Company.

as relate to the production of ectoplasm, I say nothing because I have no experience of it.

I have said more to the same purpose in *Everyman's Genius*. I have referred to it again here, chiefly to explain why mediumistic phenomena has no place in the experiences it is attempting to describe. I initiate no argument for or against the authenticity of subjective evidence, nor raise any question as to the sincerity of the investigators and the factuality of their reports. But if I admit that revelation of the past, foreknowledge of the future, disclosure of items not acquired through the intelligence, clairvoyant cognizance of contemporaneous events any or all of them are proofs of survival, then I am bound to admit that the greater part of my own work is performed by "spirits" and that my literary status is precisely that of a professional "medium." And I am not prepared to admit anything of the kind.

Years ago Henry Holt, who will be recalled as profoundly interested in these things, often did me the honor to consult me about "psychic" manuscripts which he thought of publishing. Once he asked me to report on the method and matter of Mrs. Curran, who at that time was figured in the public eye as the author of *Patience Worth* and a novel of the time of Christ, which was advertised as containing matter which could not have been acquired by ordinary methods. Mrs. Curran had written for Mr. Holt's *Unpopular Review* a straightforward account of her procedure, in which I was unable to find anything more remarkable than, or in any wise differentiated from, the procedure of any other novelist. I thought her sufficiently unusual in type to warrant study for the sake of her subjective capacity, but nothing about her work even suggested, to the habitual worker in the subconscious, the intervention of "spirits" possessed of knowledge inaccessible to the living. And that led to my saying to Mr. Holt that I had never seen any *subjective* spirit phenomena which I could not reproduce or even improve upon, by the same methods that I used every day in my own work.

Mr. Holt accordingly sent Dr. Walter Prince, at that time head of the American Psychic Research, to make the test. It turned out, however, that Doctor Prince could not have understood my challenge, for he made no sort of effort to discover what sort of safeguards would have insured the distinction between ordinary methods of utilizing the subconscious, and the use of the same medium by the dead. The only item that so much as suggested the boasted "scientific" precautions of psychic research was the pains Doctor Prince took to prevent my anticipating the answers to the questions he asked. Later Mr. Hoit told me that Doctor Prince had reported that I was a remarkable medium. I protested against the use of the term on the ground that that was what I had set out to demonstrate that I wasn't. Said Doctor Prince, "But you must be; that is the only possible explanation."

I have often wondered since whether *any* psychic researcher of that time took pains to try out the capacities of the living subconscious before assigning all such phenomena to the interpolation of the dead. Not only does my challenge still stand, to parallel any subjective evidence by ordinary means, but I could, with a little searching, produce Indians capable of doing much more. And the Indian would insist either that the evidential material was communicated to him by his totem animal, or was owing to his possession of a handful of stones and bones and nameless odds and ends carried about with him in a dirty buckskin bag.

It is not my intention to discredit the possibility that the dead may exist in a dimension which makes it feasible for them to work through the subconscious of selected living people. All that I mean to say is that the subconscious is of unknown extension, and of such varied capacity that I find it premature to determine that any of its manifestations are evidential of survival. Years ago there used to be about the West, old men whose intimate association with the land induced in them something of the responsiveness of Indians, who could be heard prefacing their attempts to communicate what they had experienced with the words "I ain't a arguin' with you, I'm just a tellin' you." What I am telling you is that though mediumistic reports may be all that you would like to believe them, they do not, so far as I am concerned, enter into the experience as related. For the reader whose own will to believe or disbelieve is so insistent that he must start an argument to protect himself from being told, this is the time to lay down the book and forget about it.

V

In 1927 Clark University instituted a conference and published a volume on *The Case for and against Psychical Belief,* to which I contributed a paper on *The Need of a Subjective Study of Death.* My idea was, that if there is such a thing as ever-livingness, it is an inherent probability of consciousness. It is something man has—as every great prophet of survival has taught—not something miraculously acquired, added to or developed out of the process of living. This does not necessarily imply that survival in complete individuality is inescapable. Every individual may not win through death any more than every conception arrives safely at birth. But the tendency toward surviving must be so natural that it could be discovered in the living human in the same way that the tendency toward and the mechanism for reproduction can be discovered and described in the adolescent human. My article urged that to begin the study of survival with supposititious messages which the discarnate were credited with sending back, reverses all our normal procedures of scientific research; that the way through death begins on *this side* and should be at least as evidential as the way back and could be recovered by studious inquiry. I was, and am still, anxious to see such a study made.

That no such study has even been properly begun is perhaps due to its extreme complexity, the delicacy of the methods that must be employed, and the necessity, if such a study is to be complete, of coordinating the work of many types of scientific research. The delay in initiating such an inquiry, in a country where money is always available for every caprice of the public mind, may also be due in some degree to the prevailing fear which, in the interim between the surrender of all belief in the Christian solution and the rise of a new prophet of survival, seems to have seized the intellectual consciousness of America. For the majority of men are, it appears, not only afraid of being afraid, they are ashamed of being caught assuaging their fear with information.

I quote from the article in question:

"Assuming that we have a right to be as logical about death as about any other human experience, let us consider whether there may not be interior evidence of the nature of death, which can be subjected to the same scientific scrutiny we have lately given to the nature of adolescence. What phenomena of the spirit, in anticipation of the crisis called death, do we observe which may be indicative of the future of that spirit in the same way that the psychology of adolescence indicates the future of the living individual?

"Inevitably such a study would concern itself with the subjective consciousness of man, with whatever part of him might be supposed to be capable of going on independently of the material frame and its purely objective existence. Such a study would normally concern itself, first of all, with the origins of consciousness, and with its modes of progression. Should the intense and scholarly inquiry which is being pursued continuously, result in any positive knowledge of the nature and origin of consciousness, it would undoubtedly be found to bear directly upon the problem of survival. But pending such illumination, in what other direction and by what methods could inquiry profitably be made? Where shall we look, in the nature of living man, what shall we look for, and by what marks shall we identify and how interpret interior evidence of the continuity of man's livingness?"

After outlining and suggesting the class of phenomena which could properly be made the subject of such study, the article closed as follows:

" . . . If death could have the undivided attention of the psychologists to the degree that the psychic reactions of the love-life have had it, would not our yield of understanding be proportionately rewarding? For death is quite as much a fact as sex, quite as likely to disguise its actuality in myths and hallucinations, myths of hauntings, of resurrections, subjective presentments of seeing and hearing.

"All this seems to me much more important than the sort of thing that is now claiming the attention of investigators. Whether or not our discarnate friends can hark backward to us over the dividing line, is relatively unimportant compared with the discovery of the quality and conditions of the adventure by which survival is accomplished.   One thing we know and one only: that if there is another existence beyond the gate of death, we go through from Here to There.   Is it not from Here, then, that the adventure can be soundly predicated?"

Many of the items so recommended for study lie in regions of human psychology so little explored as yet that there are never more than one or two scholars at a time capable of organizing such exploration.   But there are other discoveries which, if they do not come within the scope of ordinary intelligences to make, are at least verifiable to any one able to read the scholarly record of human behavior as it is written in the works of the folklorist.   The record of man's relations with the experience of death is copious and authentic.

What has lacked heretofore is an interpreter

having the key to that curious phenomena discoverable in a few of the higher quadrupeds and reaching its highest peak of expressiveness in man—I mean the phenomena of story-telling. There is a trick man has of turning his insides outside, which if it were presented to a race of beings wholly without the instinct for story-telling, would appear the most incredible of human performances. Man everywhere has a habit of creating out of scraps of his own experience, out of rag-tags of observation, out of a curious usage such things have of turning into something which is neither one of them, which, nevertheless, has in it enough of the stuff of human reality to serve as a sort of pattern reflection. The stuff that goes into these stories is not all of the sort we call actuality; some of it is the stuff of dreams, of wishful thinking, of unmeasured desires and ambitions. Much, very much of it is drawn from patterns made on the immediate consciousness by the unpremeditated motions of man's Sacred Middle; things going on so deep down in him, that he is aware only of the fact that they are going on and that they are important.

Certain experiments of mine tried out among sheep dogs on the open range, and among hunting-dogs in the process of being trained for field-trials, convinced me that the function of story-telling has rudimentary expression among them. Observations on the behavior of those little wild dogs of the wilderness, the coyotes, suggest that it may be at work even further back in the canine strain.* It is, possibly, the same thing that is observable in the kitten pretending to itself that a ball of yarn is a mouse. It is probably—this story-telling tendency—directly out of that hidden root of consciousness which works to the upper layer of expression as protective mimicry, which paints on the surfaces of the living creature, patterns with which a submerged intelligence has experimented as life-preserving probabilities. Even in man, in the earliest stages of his evolution, the story-telling instinct seems to work directly on his body to make out of him his imagined pattern of "the animal that stands up."

In the first language man invented, the gesture speech, or as it is modernly named "sign

*The Flock. Mary Austin. Houghton, Mifflin Co.

language," it is patterns of behaviors that are mainly described. The sign word for man is the finger held upright, the story of man's erect posture. The word for time is the story of a string stretched out; for eternity, an outward moving spiral. One sees the sense of pattern in behavior exteriorating itself in the string games developed by Esquimaux in the long Arctic nights, in the patterns of sticks and bones thrown in a gambling basket as an index of fortunate adventure, in the disposition of man to seek for patterns as auguries, in the entrails of his kill, in the flight of birds, the throw of cards. If you were to sit down with me to shuffle and throw any four- or six-parted deck of playing cards, I could tell you a pattern of your own personal activities which, unless you were a cleverer psychologist than I am, would surprise you with its suggestion of veracity. And that not because there is anything mystic in myself or magic in the cards, but because, being an accomplished story-teller, I know that the patterns of the cards, the "dark lady," the "person in authority," the "undeserved good fortune," the "peril of accident," were all patterns in the mind of man before ever they were extroverted in carved bones or reduced to painted figures on bits of pasteboard. And being by natural constitution a story-teller, it amuses me more to play with my folklore than to write articles upon it for encyclopedias, although I can do that too, on occasion.

In all this the fact that is pertinent to the question under discussion, is that the further you go back in the history of story-telling, the plainer it appears that what you have there is the history of man's inner awareness, the history of his knowledge-feeling, which comes through. It comes clearer in the primitive mind because primitive man has fewer intellectual conventions to take the place of unpremeditated movements of his deep-self. He plays directly with these movements rather than with the painted pasteboard presentiments of them, which are so often all that the modern man has with which to play. For this is the item that the interpretive story-teller has to take into account, that man, in his slow acquisition of the tools and technique of intelligence, has often been the loser, putting aside the animal instinctiveness on which he once successfully relied, before he has developed a really dependable mentality.

Looking, then, at the folk-knowledge of death, with all these things in mind, we seem to discover, under all the intellectual mistakes man has made about it, the inner spirit moving itself aright, to invent stories in which death will be shown in its actual nature. Although it is clear that the intelligence of man sees but one face of death, if death is an adventure in more than two dimensions the inner self should have some knowledge of it, should be able to see all around it.

The earliest notion of death that man seems to have developed, is that it is not natural; it is something that has to be accounted for. As a matter of fact, physiological science remains uncertain whether there is any such thing as "natural death," unaccounted for by illness or accident. In the beginning, a supernormal or magical origin had to be invented to satisfy man's natural curiosity. Millions of moderns still believe that man dies to-day because the first man ate a forbidden fruit, which is a figurative way of saying that somewhere in his history man did something which interfered with the natural flow of livingness.

A study of the patterns of Hereafters, of Hades and Blessed Isles, of Heaven and Hell, of hauntings and reincarnations and Happy Hunting-Grounds, reveal many versions of man's instinctive knowledge of himself, interpreted in the light of his experiential knowledge. If ever we are to discover in man an inherent capability of a life after death, it seems to me it must be somewhere within the crossing of those two sources of self-knowledge, intelligent observation and instinctive revelation. It should begin to show there, faintly as those subtle alterations in the human embryo by which the observer discovers it passing the various stages of its pre-human evolution until it arrives at unquestionable humanness.

Every now and then some superficial observer of primitive life announces that he has discovered a tribe of men wholly without any idea of a future life. What he means is that he has found them without any codified pattern of the way in which it seems to them discarnate life would proceed. If you sit long enough at their firesides you will eventually hear a story of ghostly haunting, of an ancestral spirit appearing in dreams or reincarnate in the form of an animal; or they will be reciting a rite intended to placate the soul of the quarry or the slain enemy. In the earlier stages of humanness, animals were thought of as possessing the same sort of consciousness as man; possessing, indeed, subjective powers exceeding those of man; which is a primitive way of saying that animal instincts, particularly their way-finding, food-finding, self-preservative powers generally, were originally thought of as superior to those of mankind. All discarnate spirits whether men or animals were thought of as having much the same attributes and dispositions as belonged to their physical manifestations, friendly in the case of ancestors or animals, malicious in the case of enemies. As man had occasion to think more and more of what became of spirits in the interim of doing good or doing ill to their kinsmen in the flesh, the life pictured for them was ineffectual, a land of shadows and sighs, the Hades of the Greeks, the Sand Hills of the Blackfeet.

A little later when the race had proceeded so far that there began to be a play of that curious activity called genius, there developed an idea of a somewhat more active after-life for the hero, the exceptional individual. Power was thought of as one of the characteristics most likely to survive. By this time the great natural causations had been personified and anthropomorphized into gods, always possessing that essential quality of genius, the capacity to act spontaneously in directions in which they had not been taught, to achieve results by their innate powers. This, I think, is the first note of high significance in the history of man's understanding of death. *Subjective capacity—genius—was always thought of as inherently surviving.*

It was in view of this conviction that the bodies of great men began to be preserved as fetishes, that saints were buried in the house walls and miracles worked by their remains. So it was that the imagination of man began to work on the environment of the souls of heroes. Such as these would not have deserved, they would not have endured the drab existence of Hades, the dull, occupationless everlastingness of primitive Hereafters. Is it not the uninterestingness of the Christian Heaven, with its states of stagnant ecstasy in an unvarying Hebraic environment, which has put modern man most out of humor with it?

Very early in his progressive discovery of himself, primitive man became aware of alterations of growth and aptitudes, such as changed the direction of his interior as well as exterior life. He discovered himself capable of doing things at one period of his life which he afterward abhorred. He was capable of doing things under stress which at calmer moments he felt to be detrimental. As a resolution of these contradictions within himself, he discovered the power of spiritual readjustment, which in turn gave rise to the need of a place and opportunity for such readjustments as he might have failed to make while living. His Hereafter was conceived as necessarily providing punishments and purgatories.

This is only the surface pattern of the changes that came about in man's notion of life after death. The actual root of these things is much deeper. I always start in my own speculations with that sea slug which, when it finds itself menaced, spits out its vitals, and then grows them again when the danger is past. But I realize that this is merely a dramatic incident in what was a long story, which appeals to me because of the professional importance of my own Sacred Middle. I always quake there when menaced in either my psychic or my physical existence. And when we all say, this or that "makes me sick," what do we mean but to declare our own conviction that this is chiefly what insides are for, to warn and advise and inform, to make a sensitive center from which new instrumentation can be successfully evolved.

There are two inventions in the history of man's dealing with death, for which, after years of study, I can find no *subjective* origin other than some such self-preservation instinct of consciousness itself. The first of these is the idea that death is a time of peril to the soul; that the passage from incarnate life to discarnate existence is one which requires delicate and difficult negotiation.

There is much more in this than the mere start of the life complex away from threatened disintegration. Fear of death, as we understand and experience it, scarcely appears among primitives. There is, by all reports, very little anticipatory anxiety, and no such horror as is frequent among Christians carefully tutored in the natural history of Hell. Among tribes in which the custom obtains of abandoning the aged when they are no longer able to keep up with the tribal migration, there is complete dignified acceptance. The only protest I have ever heard expressed is the song of an old woman to this effect:

> Alas that I should die now,
> I, who know so much!

But among people who have only the scantest notion of the meaning and content of life after death, there will be found rites designed to render the actual passage of death less perilous. Such rites exist in great particularity among hunting and fishing tribes, of precise but not highly developed cultures. They are found magnificently elaborated in the highest cultures of antiquity, giving rise to such carefully worked out rituals as the Egyptian *Book of the Dead,* and the Tibetan *Bardo Thödol.* In our own age the idea of death as a time of especial peril to the departing soul, persists in the Roman Catholic rite of Extreme Unction, which is of mid-Asian ancientness.

In general these rites shape themselves around a notion that the state of mind of the departing one has something to do with his successful entry into the next world. The American Indian Death Song is a typical example. The song is made out of the individual's own high moment, the peak of his perception of the meaning of Existence; he sings it before going into battle or other peril; or, dying of sickness, it is sung for him by his friends. Among many tribes, the conviction prevails that men who die in battle or women in childbirth, can read their title clear, because both these are high states of personal orientation. That is to say, they are high states originating in complete surrender to subjective impulses.

The other instinctive gesture of self-preservation made by primitive man, is the incurable gesture of expiation. To get at this we have to go back of the superficial reading of expiatory rites as a matter of bargain and sale, man bargaining with God for salvation. Something like this, in their later stages, rites of expiation became, especially when society was so far developed that it becomes habituated to accepting its religion at the hands of priests. But in its primary development, the passion of expiation connects itself with the unpremeditated movements of consciousness, and my *Holothuria* sacrificing his insides to Danger. When you think of the surrender of intricately devised instrumentation that goes on in the process of plant and animal evolution, the revising of early models, rejections and suppressions, the young man, who, in order to make a better member of a Blackfeet tribe, sacrifices the first joint of his middle finger to the Sun, is seen to be following a pattern as old as evolution, as life itself. At all times in his body he carries stumps, vestigial remainders of what life cast away. The giving up of an objective advantage for a subjective gain is a motion so universally made by man, that it must be taken into account in any summing up of the content of such instinctive gestures.

These are the concepts that are universally written into the script of man's experiential encounters with death. There are a few notations which, if not universally appearing, are of sufficiently frequent mention to deserve inclusion in the list of items that must be included. The first of these is the fact constantly being attested to by people who associate intimately with tribesmen, to the effect that primitive man can more often and more accurately foretell his own death to the day and hour, than can sophisticated man. He does so naturally, without alarm, and without any of the symptoms of that "morbidity" which sophistication is fond of attributing to any personal interest in death not characterized by horror and avoidance.

Another item to be considered is the widespread belief in the possibility of life being taken up and laid down at the will of the individual. This is the substance of a myth much older than the Christ story. Where it is not found in anthropomorphic form, there will often be a myth of the successive reappearance of animal life, in animal form. This is especially told of the great food animals, often accompanied by the idea of voluntary assumption of such form, "that the people may be fed." All such myths appear to crystallize about a concept of life as exceedingly fluent, capable of assuming any form at will.

Closely related to both the above items in the lore of death, is the further fact, of which I have no personal knowledge, but have seen stated with such assurance that I am obliged to accept it, that primitives are able to die of their own volition. If these items prove nothing, they at least suggest that formerly man had a completer access to death than is now afforded, a subjective access, a feeling-knowledge of death which enabled him to treat it as a link in a chain of experienceable probabilities.

It is this sort of universal lore of death which I should like to see ritualized in so far as it could be done without abnegating its experienceableness. If it could be done by one of those male minds that find their vocation in combing and braiding the scattered strands of reality into rational patterns called scientific, without destroying our appreciation of the fact that their validity lies in their being universally experienced, we would then possess a veracious beginning for a true study of death. The unfortunate thing about so much of the science of humanity is that it has begun with the assumption that experienceability somehow puts the material outside the range of fact.

It must be borne in mind that the range of observation of a woman of my years covers the period in which it was generally assumed by the medical profession that all the subjectively experienceable phenomena of pregnancy were to be classed as "morbid." Pregnancy itself was almost universally treated as a sickness, and its psychological manifestations as symptomatic rather than as contributive. I recall very well the smile of self-conscious superiority that, on the faces of medical men, greeted my own first suggestion that the so-called "morbid appetites" of pregnant women were genetically related to the ancient and wide-spread primitive belief that pregnancy itself was induced by the eating of strange foods, and might be considered as a completely normal effort of an immensely important subjective process to declare itself at the level of self-conscious intelligence. Even yet I would not expect a really intelligent response to such suggestion except from men of superior rank as psychologists. But it is with such items in mind that I suggest further that there may be psychological processes related to death and survival, going on in man in advance of the incident of death, of as much importance to be studied and as capable of intelligent study as are the phenomena which precede the incident of birth.

No such study is available for quotation,

not even my own. All that I can say is that
I have gone far enough in the approach to
such study to feel convinced that death may
yet be demonstrated—even without any witness from the other side—to be of the nature
of a link in experience rather than its unavoidable end.

VI

THE inquirer into the lore of death is fortunate in having at hand the written record of the convictions of men, and their methods of realizing on those convictions, in times and cultures far removed from ours. But before going into details, it seems necessary to explain why the writer feels that the subjectivity of primitive peoples is more profitable to be examined than the rationalizations of recent times. The whole business of survival is in its nature a subjective problem; the soul has never been imagined by man as inseparably identified with the sensory instrument, and opinions have always varied widely as to the extent to which the immediate intelligence enters into life after death. Many of the death rites about to be questioned are designed to save to the discarnate soul as much of its instrument as is thought likely to serve him in the life to come. The whole trend of funerary customs indicates a belief that, as the discarnate soul proceeds on its way, it is more and more able to dispense with the tools and appurtenances so necessary to this life. And all its appeals and reappearances to those who are left behind, are so universally recognized as subjective in their character, that veridical appearances—what we would call hallucinations—are usually accepted as warnings of disaster. The walking of the ancestral ghost, the wailing of the family banshee, the appearance of the guardian saint or angel, sometimes the persistent experience of the sense of presences, are still taken to intimate that the percipient is himself about to enter into that state which the appearances imply.

It is unfortunate for the purposes of this inquiry that there is no study adequately covering that period of man's development during which he was in process of escape from the almost complete subjectivity of his animality, and began to depend, for his major processes, on intellectualization. I have already suggested that this was a period in which considerable loss occurred, which, on the part of the great mass of mankind, has never been made up. As animals, great numbers of men are less

successful than many of their four-footed ancestry, and as rational beings fail even more
completely. Perhaps it would not be too much
to say that the majority of human beings everywhere, having lost the decisive knowledge-feeling of animals, without attaining to a very
reliable mentality, are sustained by dependence
upon intellectual tradition organized under the
general term of education. They spend their
lives, as it were, going over a Brooklyn bridge
of intellectual tradition, not having thought
out for themselves a single one of the primary
principles or practical processes involved in its
construction.

But there was a time when the bridge by
which human society crossed from animality
to intellectuality, was built up out of a tradition of subjective processes whose roots were in
the instinctive and automatic behaviors of our
animal ancestry. Since these are the actual
processes by which life attained to self-
conscious humanism, it always seems to me
they are immensely worth questioning for news
of man's destiny. At this time the race had
not yet developed that exaggerated notion of

the value of intellectualization which obsesses
the common man of to-day. The Dawn-man's
intellectual explanation of his experience was
naïve and much more easily separated from
the essential processes of his deep-self. Taking man as he presents himself in the period
after the use of fire had been acquired, and
before the bow had been invented, on through
the hunting cultures to the settled agricultural
community cultures, we find his subjective life
definitely characterized by traits that must be
taken into account in the unraveling of his attitude toward death and survival.

At that time the passage from intellectualization to subjectivity was much more readily affected, facilitated, no doubt, by the absence
of those intellectual prejudices against subjective experience, which later served to divide
man from his superstitions. Early man knew
that his subjectively acquired knowledge was
worth more to him on most matters, than his
intellectual observation. He believed his
dreams, acted on his hunches, accepted the
promptings of genius as of supernormal origin.
He dreamed easily and vividly, like a child,

and there is no doubt in my mind that his dreams did have a closer relation to actuality than do the dreams of man constantly impinged upon by the racket of civilized life. Primitive man relied upon his dreams, asked for them, and the subconscious life in him answered after a way it has, when called upon. The universal vestigial remainder of this practise expressed in modern man's desire to "sleep on the proposition," testifies to the earlier authenticity of this type of partially submerged activity.

In primitive man, that whole range of sensitivities about way-finding, mate-finding and the food-search, of which the modern "hunch" is the survival, were not only more acute, but of immense direct importance to the survival of particular groups. The play of genius, by which I mean the irruption of ancestrally acquired capabilities into the immediate life of the individual, was quicker and more generally distributed, naturally freer from acquired prejudices and insufficiently grounded notions about genius.

Then there is that group of capacities for foreseeing the future, uncovering the past, revealing the unseen, which appears in all primitive societies, and under such fearsome names as cryptesthesia, telekinesis and psychometry is now being readmitted to respectable society. Since several good books on these so-called Supernormal Faculties, as they persist in modern life, have already appeared, there is no necessity of saying more than that they may also be found actively in use among American aboriginals, where I have personal experience of them. But because they are used by aboriginals they are not necessarily free from that curious liability I have before referred to as sleight of mind; nor can I entirely separate them from similar phenomena that occur in connection with the normal process of creative composition, especially story-telling. My own private conviction is that most, if not all of these manifestations, can be successfully rationalized only when we have completely resolved the whole problem of genius. The immediate point is that all these things occur with reasonable dependability in the psychic life of early man, and that they are not there accepted as evidence of survival. When they occur without dramatization—that is to say without vision or hallucination, either optical or auditory—they are usually attributed to the Ancestors, not as individual tribal ghosts but as a group *wakonda*. When dramatized, they are almost invariably referred to the Totem Animal, or the Animal Helper. That is to say they involve a concept of unbroken continuity in consciousness.

When I make statements like that about how primitive man thinks of what we are accustomed to call psychological problems, I am drawing upon my knowledge of how primitive man behaves in the presence of such problems, rather than upon how he formulates his thinking about them. Everywhere in the oldest folklore, one comes upon evidence that the Dawn-man assumed the same sort of consciousness in himself and in other animals, and that the ascendent tribes have retained some sort of traditional memory of creatures that were more animal than men, and that yet aspired to the status of mankind. There were innumerable tales to show that early man realized that animals possessed powers of sense or of intuition which man had lost, but could repossess through the tuition or guardianship of a friendly animal. Thus it could be easily shown that man came into a realization of his manness out of a state in which it was normally assumed that the passage in and out of the condition called death was common to both men and animals. Life could be laid down; it could be taken up again. It was not inevitable that the same *form,* the same garment of life, be assumed. In dealing with Indian tales I have often to remonstrate on the implications of cruelty that are read into tales of the killing of one creature by another, especially in the Trickster cycles. Actually these are in the nature of such practical joking as occurs when one boy steals the clothes of a comrade in swimming. The real creature turns up again uninjured, having put on another suit of personality. These tales are not told to prove that life is indestructible, but because it is taken for granted that it is so.

Of all other psychic phenomena which may be thought of as entering into this discussion, every possible type seems to be represented in tribal man. Indeed, I should say that hunting

man has more actual knowledge of the motions of his own psyche than the average man
in the street. Quite certainly he is able to make
better use of them. Since a scientist of the
standing of J. W. Dunne has shown in *An
Experiment with Time* how easily the faculty
of dreaming true can be restored to intellectual
man, I may add that I have tried out in my
own practise every psychic device discovered
among American Indians, and find them superior in most cases to what was known by the
general public twenty-five years ago. Experiments in hypnotism at the School of Nancy
have been carried out with more particularity
than among Indians, but with no different results. Among most tribes, suggestion is practised with high specialization, although still
explained as magic. Greater use of hypnoidal
states is made, especially in healing, and the
Amerind use of rhythm for healing and for
raising the plane of group activity is far in advance of anything of ours. Here in my immediate neighborhood, a form of crystal-gazing
is practised by means of water poured into a
black pottery bowl. Hypnotics and vision-

producing drugs are used.   Possibly because
of its association with the still magical properties of fire, smoke is almost universally employed to induce profitable mental states, particularly tobacco smoke.

There are remarkably fine discriminations
among the tribesmen in the use of psychic
methods, but in talking with medicine men, no
corresponding discriminations of definition can
be discovered.   They distinguish always between an induced "vision" and an hallucinatory
vision, but not between hallucination and reality.   Thus, they know that the Ancestral Spirit,
or Totemic Animal evoked by rites, is not actual, but they think the apparition of a dead
friend who comes to warn of approaching
death, is actual.   Nor do they distinguish between veridical death and any form of complete
unconsciousness.   Said an Indian to me not long
ago, describing what happened to him at an
important initiation, "And then I died for a
little while," meaning simply that he fainted
as the result of an exacting ritual following a
long fast.

I may say here that Indians pass rather

easily into conditions of trance and other states known to our own mystics as meditation, contemplation and various states of detachment. It has occurred to me that these things are fundamentally related to behaviors of lower life forms: hibernation, pupation, "playing possum," protective mimicry and all the various devices by which less evolved life forms evade disaster by temporary regressions into still earlier forms. But I do not mean that these states, estimated as states of consciousness, are to be called "lower" and so considered negligible. I mean that the power to assume these states is one of the things we have relinquished on the way to become rational beings. Once it has become enmeshed in the more complex instrument necessary to intelligence, consciousness can not perform all its earlier tricks. It can not restore a human arm as it could a starfish arm, but it can and does often perform marvelous reconstructions of delicate tissue. It can not melt down the body stuff and after an interval reform it on an entirely different pattern as in the case of the Lepidoptera, but it can do other things strongly reminiscent of

its earlier capacities, especially if it first re-
gresses into simulacra of pupation and hibernation, through trance and hypnosis. Primitive
man, at any rate, seems to have early made an
empirical discovery of the preservative use
that can be made of such retrogressive states
when self-induced.

These things have profoundly influenced
man's notions of survival, and are still to be
discussed in his important religions, and are
mentioned here because they are for ever present as experience in my own mind, influencing
my interpretations, even when not expressly
mentioned.

VII

ALL primitive religions have so much that is universally fundamental and locally various, that it seems important merely to resurvey rapidly those fundamentals. These are seen ordinarily to revolve around and grow out of two concepts, in full possession of which man appears within the ken of history.

The first of these is the profound affirmation of the soul as a separable item of man's constitution; and the second is of the indestructible quality of the soul. Frazer says of the Melanesian, that belief in ever-livingness "is an inbred, unquestioning, omnipresent conviction which affects his thoughts and actions at every turn." Of the Bantu, Sir Wallace Budge declares that they "appear to have no belief in gods apart from ghosts and ancestral influences."

Death is regarded as an intrusion, needing to be accounted for by a myth. The dead are thought of as more mysterious and powerful than the living, but requiring to be nourished and sustained, at least through the early stages of their journey, in much the same way as the living. Moustierian man, an early European type, of whom we know little else, buried his dead with tools and weapons and food for continued existence.

Death is not feared in these early religions, but the dead are esteemed fearful, and funerary customs are mingled with rites for placating the dead and keeping them friendly. Their interest in the living was retained and attention reciprocated. They could be called up, and very early there developed the notion that there were special places propitious to this, and special people successful at it.

The dead were supposed to be attached to localities and given to haunting the place of their departure at first, later setting out for the Land of the Hereafter, which was never very specifically defined or described. Two distinct tendencies of intellectual origin were noted: one to destroy the body to facilitate departure, and the other to preserve it, lest it be required for use again.

The act of death was thought of as a time

of peril for the soul, more or less guarded against either by death rites or by later rites performed by the friends.

All of these postulates about death seem to have arisen before there was any well-developed theology, or even a clearly defined anthropomorphism of the various aspects of life and nature by which man felt himself worked upon. There is not lacking evidence in many cases of gods arising—and arising directly—out of ancestor worship.

Practically all the things that were believed about human survival were held to be true of animal survival. Rites for placating the spirits of the quarry were co-existent with rites for humans having the same significance.

Upon these general postulates all Occidental notions of death, of heaven and hell and judgment were later erected. In the majority of cases, tribal religions were more affected by death concepts than ideas of death were influenced by religion. It was the nature of the life after death that was most influenced by concepts of gods and god-homes. The bringing of the dead and the gods together, through their common indestructible mysteriousness, marks the end of the period that can be called primitive.

Fortunately one of the greatest and most homogeneous civilizations of antiquity has left us an account of its dealing with death and its corollary of survival, in complete particularity. The Egyptians appear upon the scene of history with a cult of survival so completely accepted that it became the organiz'ng center of their social and cultural life. Death was a crisis in a continuous cycle of livingness conceived of as inherently indestructible, so that a man's funeral was often the most important event in his life. All the Egyptian's religious thought centered about the act of leaving this life and entering the next. Rites were invented for every possible contingency that might arise in a Hereafter which was more explicitly mapped than any other unless it be the Hereafter of Medieval Christianity. This other world was thought of as so complicated that the newly arrived soul required a guide-book to avoid disaster. In this book were found all possible traveler's directions, words of power, formulas, pictures of gods by which they might be instantly recognized, lists of important names and much good advice.

The Egyptian idea of the soul was complex, though probably not more so than the idea modern man has of his own inner constitution, especially if he makes a stab at self-knowledge in the light of the new psychology. There was a self of which the soul, or *sahu,* was a swift, shining, indestructible replica, powerful and free; not thought of as complete without its *khaibit* or shadow. There was the *ka,* probably an earlier form of the "double," which remained in this life, usually accommodated in the tomb, and had a kind of independent life of its own, at least so long as the body retained its identity. Then there was a separable element, called the *ba* which might enter into other bodies, so that a living man might become the host of several *ba* not his own. There was the *ab,* the sum of passions and emotions, and finally there was the *khu,* or soul of the spirit. Out of this complexity of concept grew the intricate ritual of death and the cult of the preservation of the body for which Egypt is distinguished among the nations. The body must be preserved for the sake of the *ka,* to be the vehicle of its special prerogative of "coming forth by day." The tomb must be decorated and furnished to make the *ka* feel at home, and in anticipation of future possibilities, in which the self was somewhat vaguely pictured as revisiting the glimpses of the moon.

The special time of peril for the discarnate soul was the Judgment, which took place immediately after the dead had been ferried across the Dark River. It is said that certain of these dead ones whose passports were not in order, spent the whole of their after-life being carried back and forth, as houseless unfortunates could once be found spending the night on the Hoboken ferry. The Judgment took place in the Hall of Judgment, in the presence of certain of the elder gods, and its special feature was the weighing of the soul; holdings in the Hereafter being measured by deserts. Once safely past this ordeal, the traveler wandered about the other world, having many adventures, for which the *Book of the Dead* provided him with safeguards and instruction, and ultimately came face to face with the great gods and claimed participation in their nature.

The dominating religious feature of Egyptian death rites was the cult of Osiris. This Osiris is presumed by many scholars to have been originally a man who, like Jesus, taught, suffered and died and gave a convincing appearance of return in the flesh. As with Christianity, the spiritual achievement of Egyptian religion is the demonstrable power of life over death. The dead were named, ceremonially, The Triumphant.

The Egyptian *Book of the Dead,* a copy of which was frequently put into the sarcophagus or painted on to the walls of the tomb, dealt wholly with the conduct of the soul after death. The Tibetan *Book of the Dead,* the *Bardo Thödol,* since it treated of the art of dying, was left in the hands of the friends of the departed. It arose out of the religious complex that goes by the name of Buddhism, of which the central idea is that no death is natural in the sense that it is inevitable to occur without lesion or malady. The generating force of

Buddhism is the idea that life consists of a series of successive states of consciousness, of which the goal is Buddhahood, that is to say, complete illumination, such as makes possible the final reabsorption of the spiritual entity into the Void, or Nirvana.

Buddhism and Brahmanism, the two Oriental religions most akin, are, at first glance, so complicated as to daunt the unaccustomed Occidental mind. They are, as a matter of fact, singularly apt and direct examples of religions that, starting with the unpremeditated idea of life as successive states of consciousness, go spiraling outward, generating, as they go, vast abstractions, macrocosmic philosophical concepts, until they gather the universe into their majestic sweep. Also by the very force of their goingness they gather up and carry with them a great variety of lesser concepts, such as arise in the intellectual life of successive epochs, such as are added to the sum of social concepts by conquests and alliances and tribal exchanges; gods and demons, rites, moralities, decadencies and picturesque behaviors. These ride the spiral as dead leaves and dust particles the whirlwind, dropping back at last, to leave the generating idea of life as successive states of consciousness, climbing the Void, rid of its incidental encumbrances.

Buddhism distinguishes itself initially from the religions which are still contemporaneous with it, by conceiving the soul not as a compact entity, as is the case with Islam and Christianity, but rather as "a complex of activities, psychical and physical, having life as their function." This complex is thought of as in instant change, a series of momentary states, generated, the one from the other, a continuous transformation. To none of the states is death an absolute ending; but to all it occasions the separation of the psyche from the physical body, and at the same time provides a bridge to another term of physical existence by which another step is accomplished in the stair that leads to Buddhahood. While the soul-complex is thought of as able to hold together of its own inherency, the need of some sort of body in which to acquire merit by experience, is always felt. The Tibetan concept is of an intermediate state between the death of one body and the reestablishment of the soul-complex in another about to be born. This intermediate state is called a *Bardo,* and is normally supposed to last about fifteen days. (Very advanced souls are said to be capable of simply abandoning a used body of their own volition, without the necessary defibrinating process of illness.) The *Bardo Thödol* is a book of instruction by which the passage from one reincarnation to another may be made in the most advantageous manner.

Every good Tibetan is supposed to have familiarized himself with the contents of the book during his life. When the symptoms of death begin to appear, a teacher, a disciple or a friend recalls it to him by reading or reciting. It is thought particularly advantageous for the dying one to reach his end in a high state of awareness, and certain practises are introduced to keep him in this state to the last, with his consciousness rightly directed. After physical death has ensued the body is removed, and the reading and reciting goes on by calling up the image of the departed, and directing the instruction toward it. The special peril supposed to be undergone is that of losing spiritual detachment—it is especially advised that there should be no wailing of the "fond mate" or family of the dying one during the instruction—and so falling into Hell, or failing to make a wise selection of the new life into which to be reborn. During the *Bardo* there will be distracting and fearsome hallucinatory apparitions—Oriental demons really make our own Satan appear a little tin devil of a fellow—which the discarnate soul is advised to regard steadily as reflections of his own thought-forms, having no more reality than the reflection of the moon in water. The instruction, prayers, formulas and rites go on until the discarnate one is supposed to be safely shut up in the womb of a new birth. The penalty of failure in the *Bardo* is that of being born again after much difficulty, into one of the lower forms of life, and so losing valuable time on the way to Buddhahood.

Christianity is unique among important religions, as the only one which rooted itself in a social organism without any well-defined notion of the soul and its inherent capacities. Judaism founded itself on the concept of one tribal god, first thought of as superior to all other gods, and somewhat later as being the only deity with an actual existence. Although in the religious history of the Jews, there are intimations of a popular belief in survival—as in the case of the Witch of Endor who raised up spirits—the idea was never incorporated among its essential orthodoxies. Jesus, when he came, found his co-religionists divided into two sects, one of which believed, and the other denied, the principle of individual survival. Without giving us any clue to his approach, Jesus appears fully possessed of the idea of the soul's immortal quality.

His teaching is filled with the concept of the separable soul as the important item in the make-up of mortal man. But he conceives of the soul as an entity and its life planes as two, here and hereafter. To what extent he believed that what happens to man in the little span of physical life, determines once and for all its status in eternity, it is not easy to discover. All that he said concerning the soul, its relation to deity, to the Hereafter, and the nature of that

Hereafter, is compressed into something less than two thousand words. And that includes all the parables that bore upon the subject and all that was said in reference to the Kingdom on earth, which in the beginning of his teaching he expected to happen in his lifetime. What is certain is that he regarded the alteration from this life to the next as something that could happen quite simply and directly, without necessarily involving any upsetting conditions. We have no reason to believe that he emphasized resurrection of the body, although he appears to have accepted complete personal identity after death. Later, it was the Jewish resistance to this idea of personal immortality which confused his teaching by putting off immortality until the resurrection.

Jesus' own expressed idea was that ever-livingness is inherent, man *hath* eternal life. There is no hint, in his teaching, of death as a time of special peril, rather, a swift release into higher and freer spiritual activity, the child let out from school. He confronted his own crisis with dignity and grace, faltering only in the instant when the tortured body failed, and was

not thrown out of poise by the singular circumstance of finding himself again more than
thirty hours afterward, in the flesh. But to
direct question, on the part of his disciples, as
to the organization and mode of life hereafter,
he replied chiefly by explaining that it was not
what they thought it was.

The contribution which Jesus made to our
ideas of the future of life was mainly as to the
place of God in that life, and the soul's relation
to divinity. Up to Jesus' time, European
thought had constituted the gods, in nature and
attributes, apart from man, but Jesus taught
them as one stuff even as the father is of one
stuff with his son, and every man a son of God,
inherently. He taught that God is Spirit, in
a sense that only recently we have been able to
understand. He taught a mystical union of
the divinity in man with the Spirit which is
God, and that the chief of man's religious activities was to maintain this union at as high and
consistent a level as lay within his capacity.
He taught that there was a spirit that could
be called into play to effect this union, a holy,
whole-making spirit. He taught this mystical

union, this liaison with God by means of the Holy Ghost, as the indispensable condition to a successful survival. These things were possible because God is Spirit—omnipresent, omniscient, omnipotent, everlasting Spirit; neither a person nor a reflection of man's thought-forms, but a fundamental reality, the Universal Consciousness to whom man is related by states of consciousness.

It seems probable that Jesus meant his disciples to understand that by the absence of this mystical union, man's possibilities of survival were menaced. At least they so understood him, believing later that death of the spirit might be the wages of whatever behaviors divided them from mystical union with God, and eternal punishment the penalty of deliberate choice or cherishing of the behaviors and states of mind inimical to such union. But of the Hell which he mentioned incidentally as though it were no great matter, needing no particular explication, it is certain Jesus meant no such place of ingenious everlasting torture as was later imagined.

Nor did he particularize about the Heaven

of the Kingdom, other than to reassure his disciples as to its being able to accommodate more than the children of Abraham, and more various spiritual capabilities than his immediate followers thought likely. And more than any prophet of immortality of like following, he avoided explicit directions for attaining it.

There are several reasons for the lack of ritual and other psychological aids, for aspirants to the Heaven of Jesus. One of them, no doubt, is the short period of his teaching—much less than the three years formerly ascribed to it. Another was the character of his disciples who desired a social revolution more than they did a mystical union with God, and continually disappointed him with their failure to realize his kingdom as not of this earth. But perhaps the greatest reason is to be found in the attitude of Jesus himself toward ritual and the processes of spiritual growth.

He thought of the "kingdom" in man as being inherent, natural as the growth of the seed in the ground; he thought of that growth as going on in man of its own motion, and capable of being trusted as seed is trusted. If ritual and rites helped you, good; if not, why bother? It is also probable, that having become habituated to such practises favorable to spiritual growth as were used by the Essenes, he thought of them as easily accessible to his hearers, as were the sacrificial rites of the Jewish religion, some of which he observed. He also submitted to the newly introduced rite of baptism, but did not practise it upon his following. That he was acquainted with, and probably adept at, a system of mystical approach to Divine Union, seems likely from references in the Gospel of St. John. But all in all, few religions destined to so wide an acceptance, have been launched with so little of explicit instruction for the use of dumb and yearning souls.

I can not suppose that it will strike across the mind of to-day as sharply as it did on mine half a lifetime ago, to discover how much of the saving ritual of Christianity, how much of the technique of the inner life, was borrowed from the great pagan faiths of the past, and how much of doctrine developed out of roots of belief planted in the minds of tribal man by—and this is the saving grace of such borrowings—*experiences* of the Dawn-mind. As if, having come to the wedding feast of the Heavenly Bridegroom without the requisite wedding garment, early Christianity had searched not only the hedges and highways, but the Royal Roads, the throne rooms of palaces and the sanctuaries of temples, that it might be appropriately dressed.

I do not now refer merely to such obvious reconstitutions as the Roman Hierarchy, nor to the substitution of the Jewish Lamb of the Sacrifice for the simple submission of the prophet to mob stupidity. Those things, like the story of the Nativity and the eating of the body of the God in the Sacrament, were transcripts of true religious gestures out of one language into another. What I have in mind is the way in which Christianity took over the ascetic practises flourishing in Egypt and made out of them monastic orders, from which grew—along with many tares—the fine wheat of the technique of prayer and the mystic approach.   I am thinking of how the Church, lacking any ritualistic approach to death as prescribed by the founder of its religion, reached into Asia Minor for the rite of Extreme Unction; gathered up from the Far East and the southern shore of the Mediterranean practises of Masses for the Departed, and other rites out of which issued the Communion of the Blessed Dead; how in the places left empty by the homely gods of the farm and the market-place, they established the kindly accessible saints.

I must not be misunderstood to say more than I mean.   The Saints are exemplars of the virtues that distinguished them in life, even as boundary stones are exemplars of the virtues required of such; but the Saints are virtues come to expressiveness in man . . . linking man to God by their godliness and God to man by their humanity.   One accepts the reasonableness of their being there, where, as intermediaries and intercessors, if we are to accept the continuity of consciousness, great and illumined souls might well be.   I can believe in Saints.   I am good at believing so long as you agree with me that all beliefs are projections on the intellectual plane of that inknowing which is a normal function of consciousness.

I can equally believe the Hell which assembled itself—as a concept of the torment of discarnate consciousness which has missed its step—in the mind of Dante, out of dim Etruscan and Orphic and Egyptian as well as Semitic surmises. Nor would I pass these things over lightly, without offering evidence of their factuality, were it not to hurry on to say that what I finally discovered behind the structure of Christianity at its peak of notability, is practically all that was genuinely experienceable of the great pagan religions. By the end of its first thousand years, the Church left off being a merely tribal or racial religion and became the repository of all the most valuable spiritual remainders of western peoples.

I was a long time coming to these conclusions, so long and at such pains that at last I felt obliged to write a life of Jesus*, as a way of making my work seem somehow more important than the goal of a private search. And immediately after, I began to understand why

*A Small Town Man. Mary Austin. Harper's.

I hadn't been able to find a Protestant anywhere who could talk to me intelligently about
the technique of prayer.

The only technique of prayer the Western
World has ever produced is that one to which
Egypt and Greece, and especially Rome, had
contributed out of treasured experience, which
was developed and carried forward to the point
at which modern psychology now resumes the
work, through the lives and labors of the Christian mystics.

I shall come back to that a little later. All
I am trying to do now is to map, in the briefest
possible way, the ground covered by my own
study during the years in which the new psychology was reforming itself on the knowledge
of the subjective consciousness in the individual.

VIII

CONCERNED as I am to keep this narrative within experienceable bounds, it has been necessary to make a detour into the way of religions, because one of the most exciting and generally profitable of my personal adventures has been the experiencing of religions. Although most people who read books of this sort are familiar with the history and dogmas of the principal world religions, if there is one thing that the modern intellectual knows less of than another, it is the true inwardness of any religion, *as psychological experience.* Here in the United States it has become more impossible than anywhere in the world to discuss these matters, because the vocabulary of the Saints—the only one Europe ever had—is a dead language here, and the vocabulary of the new psychology is still too friable to support any sound body of spiritual doctrine.

The mistake, of course, is in thinking you have to "accept" a religion to get any good out of it. All you have to do is to use it. Properly

used, the psychological activities which under-
lie all religious forms, become immensely in-
structive. I say forms instead of doctrines,
since the latter term is now generally used for
the intellectual explanations of religious beliefs; and intellectual explanations of the intuitive starts of the religious instinct are more
often and more extensively mistaken than are
the explanations of science. Whenever I want
to experience a new religion, I try to discover
its primary concepts in relation to the movements of man's Sacred Middle, which set them
going. I search out the spiritual objectives
arising from such concepts, and the technique
by which they are supposed to be attained.

Then I set about experiencing them precisely as I would a daily dozen or a problem
in dynamic symmetry. I do not bother about
belief, because I know that if the thing works
out for true, I shall end by believing it; and
I take no account of the attached moralities,
since wherever a morality is genetically related
to a spiritual concept I shan't be able to escape
it.

This sort of thing began with me when I

was very young, being disposed, as has already been described, to religious exercises. It took on connotations of intellectual importance in the early twenties, when I found myself in a situation the worst imaginable for one of my temperament, intelligence and endowment. I needed help out of the ordinary, and was, at the time, furthest removed from any possible source of such help as might be ordinarily available. And I couldn't find it in the Protestant sect in which I had been brought up.

The trouble with Protestantism in general is, that in its anxiety to return to the simpler teaching of Jesus by ridding itself of the borrowings and adaptations from defunct pagan religions, it threw away fifteen centuries of the technique of spiritual achievement. And having also discarded symbolism, which is the only competent vocabulary of the spiritually inexpressible, and rejected Roman ritual, Protestantism never succeeded in acquiring enough of its own. Getting no help from my inherited religion, I turned to the nearest at hand, which was one of the simplest forms of tribal practise.

To my surprise, I found that a serious practise of the religion of the Paiutes did for me
exactly what they claimed it would; it met my
need in so far as that need was confined within
the range of tribal experience. You can't expect a primitive religion to answer for the
innermost needs of twentieth-century sophistication; but it was interesting to discover how
like the tribal necessities certain requirements
of sophistication can be. The Paiutes believed
in something called The-Friend-of-the-Soul-
of-Man, not a person, but available for help.
They taught me all the ways they knew of
reaching it, and for the exigencies for which
their method was designed, it worked.

Greatly cheered, I went on practising tribal
religions in an ascending scale, as fast as I
could discover them. I found that where
Methodism had failed to help my inescapable
urge toward literary expression, even menaced
it by weighting it with outworn moral obligations, Indian religions went simply and directly
to the source, showing me how to escape the
trammels of a single form, and play as readily
into one literary mode as another.

About that time a chance meeting with the admired William James opened the way for understanding the intimate interrelations of religion and genius, through the subconscious. Let me be entirely honest. I called it chance then, but I know now that any such profound and single-minded desire as mine, acts somewhat as the homing instinct of a pigeon, and leads to natural satisfactions. I went along for several years with what I had from William James, and what came to me by way of my studies in folklore, for the method of which, turning me in the precise direction I would have wished to go, I am indebted to another "chance" meeting with Frederick Webb Hodge. I was at that age where one takes experts seriously, and Mr. Hodge told me how to handle folklore so that it nourished me. The same sort of chance led me to cross the Atlantic on the same steamer with just the Italian Prince who could introduce me favorably to the eminent and incredibly brilliant Cardinal Merry del Val, under whose tutelage I began to experience the religion of early Roman Christianity, and was finally introduced to the Saints.

The first books I read, opening up to me the Mystic Way of the three great centuries of Christian faith, were loaned to me out of the Cardinal's private library, and the only instruction I ever had in the technique of Christian prayer came from Mother Veronica of the Blue Nuns to whom the Cardinal introduced me. There was also a little parish priest in a patched cassock, reported to have such power in prayer that the then Pope often employed him on projects dear to his heart, who taught me how to recognize submerged errors in the method of direct prayer; and later there was a distinguished Jesuit who inducted me into the spiritual exercises of St. Ignatius. No, they did not trouble me with questions of belief; they knew that I had all the belief that is really necessary, the belief that man's situation in the universe is not hopeless, and that the means of help lie in the natural motions—intelligently directed— of his own soul. Perhaps they knew, being deeply versed in the Church that, more than any other, makes a fetish of belief, that it is chiefly the necessity of belief that Church organization imposes, which stands in the way of

religion being understood. I never inquired.
There was greatness in their attitude toward
me, giving without asking. Not for worlds
would I breathe upon the bright surfaces of
their spiritual loyalties.

Three years later in England I listened to
Swamis, and one extraordinarily able teacher
of the Raga Yoga. Yoga is a system of yok-
ing up the lower, human nature to the higher,
divine nature in such a manner that the higher
can direct the lower. Its practise consists
chiefly of psychophysical exercises, of which
the explanation is, to our Occidental notion,
grotesque, and its practical results amazing. I
still use certain selected Yoga exercises, but
charily. I never went so far in the practise as
to be able to do what one Yoga offered to do,
swallow five different-colored handkerchiefs
rolled into balls and then vomit them forth in
any desired order; but far enough to realize
that its claims are not extravagant, however
unrelated to any of my needs.

Afterward I went through the religion of
pre-Christian Rome, from which the early
church borrowed so much, and found it remark-

ably adapted to material exigencies. And so on to the Greek, whose subtleties often escaped me, although every now and then I have another try at them. And that is what I mean by experiencing religions. I kept note-books, and discovered much that is not in print—unless I have put it there*—but is present in the back of my mind informing the situation of the hour.

The Dawn-man's unargued assumption is that there is some kind of life-power in every created thing, capable of being exercised by that thing, of being sent forth by it, helpfully or harmfully to the observer. This we call by any one of its local names, *orenda* or *wakonda,* as accounting for any of the inexplicable phenomena of things—a rock glittering in the late light, a bird singing, a buffalo affecting the hunter with the sense of mysterious awe, are all exercising their *wakonda*; so is a man making a song, or following a hunch. If then, the religious rite one is about to perform, concerns a Thing, the business of the participant is to

Everyman's Genius. Mary Austin. Bobbs-Merrill Company.

put his own *wakonda* into sympathy with the *wakonda* of the Thing—say the great corn plant, exercising its *wakonda* by growing and bourgeoning in the sun—in such a way that the *wakonda* of the needy man may work persuasively or compellingly on the Thing. It must be borne in mind that this desirable liaison between the *wakonda* of the man and the *wakonda* of the corn is, even when secured by objective means, a state of consciousness.

The Dawn-man's earliest way of getting into the inner consciousness of the corn, so as to make it work for him, is by what is called sympathetic magic, doing what it does, learning to understand the universe by getting inside it. What you have to do to follow the working of its *wakonda* is to pose yourself as the corn, and imitate it, making use of that mimetic faculty, so acutely exercised in protective mimicry, of which man the animal comes into the world possessed. This is not a mystical statement: it is one of the inescapable matters of fact of animal life, the animal making himself safe by assimilating his appearance to that aspect of the universe to which he is nearest. Man has lost the trick of so doing except by a conscious process called dramatization. You dramatize the corn plant as it is, in order that you may go on from that to dramatize it as you wish it to be. Every possible aid to such dramatization may be utilized, painting your body in summer colors, building a head-dress to typify the summer landscape and the hill horizon, decorating yourself with white-cloud feathers and suggesting the sound of welcome rain with pebbled gourds and deer-hoof rattles. And, since it is so well understood that what is to be achieved is a state of consciousness, nothing known to affect the consciousness favorably is neglected. Most primitive rites are preceded by periods of preparation which involve apartness; any or all the traditional means of fasting, continence, meditation, prayer and sometimes sacrifice and pain. Having tried all of them I find that I, personally, get no particular aid to the necessary detachment through physical asceticism. Fasting never gives me the clear-mindedness other people report; I suffer much, grow dizzy and finally faint. But there is a certain continence of mind and emotion which is indispensable. Detaching oneself by any available means from all human involvements is, for me, as necessary a preparation for effective prayer as it is for writing a poem.

None of these preludes to religious rites have been so much misunderstood as the use of sacrifice and pain. The affective value of sacrifice lies only in securing detachment, as you do often when you sacrifice something in connection with which there is an involved emotional release. The office of pain as a prelude to an increased religious consciousness, is that in learning to endure pain without flinching, the neophyte is pushed into states of consciousness which are beyond pain. In convents where I have been received often for that Catholic practise known as "retreat," I have found pain used to secure concentration when there is protracted "dryness," a condition well known to those professionally devoted to a life of prayer. To know how that works, the curious might try kneeling on a broomstick, taking flight from the torment as I did into my blue spark. It must be borne in mind that pain is merely a stupid waste of energy unless one succeeds in rising upon it as on a stair. The slogan one heard so often during the late war, "Give till it hurts," is as silly as most slogans, unless the giving actually affords spiritual release, and the hurt drives the tortured consciousness along the road to a desired goal of detachment and consequent spiritual enlargement.

Some primitives use narcotics to provoke the desired states, but I happened to have no occasion for such experimentation. The use of smoke as an aid to meditation, through its hypnotic influence, is well known and widely practised. Other devices which the Indians, among whom I learned these things, use freely, are dancing, music and rhythm. Of these I find the Pyrrhic rhythm of the Medicine Drum, a steady, quick but unhurried and absolutely unaccented beat, remarkably effective. After twenty-four hours of it, practically uninterrupted, especially when it comes from the underground kivas, I find myself in a state of mental poise and lucidity not attained in any other fashion. I am inclined to believe that certain physical conditions are greatly improved thereby.

When the careful performance of all the psychological conditions has been coordinated into a ritual by that form of subconscious activity which we recognize as giving rise to results called "art," then, at the very peak of the performance, occurs the effective wish. This may be expressed in words, in gestures, or in the moment of pregnant silence which many rites afford. There is such a moment connected with the Hunting Ceremonies of the Rio Grande Pueblos, in which the whole village consummates a fruitful relation to the increase-making Powers, of which I am not prepared to say that the petition so presented does not get the inclusive response that the tribesman confidently expects of it. And yet I have known people who take seriously the elevation of the Host, and think the three-minute silence of Armistice day both moving and effective, who are astonished at my own reverent participation in a pagan ceremony.

In experiencing the religion of the ancient Romans, one is again dealing with a primitive concept, which is, that every Thing, and every cluster of natural forces presenting itself phenomenally as a whole, such as a thunder-storm or a harvest, has its essential inwardness, its spirit, or essence, which also is possessed of outgoing power similar to the *wakonda* of the western tribesmen. There is more anthropomorphism in the Roman religion than in the Amerind:—Pomona who loves the orchard and Liber, the vine, Pales for the cattle-shed, and an active principle of fertilization for the dung heap.

Even the boundary stone at the corners of the fields is capable of being acted upon favorably by libations. The good Roman had only to observe certain ritualistic acts, mostly of suggestive value, and to recite certain prayers which are chiefly affirmative in form, to keep himself in harmony with the working forces of nature. The great, the utterly mysterious forces of nature and human destiny were more highly personalized, but the psychological nature of the rites performed in their honor was scarcely different from the rites of the dung heap and the boundary stone. Sacrifice to them became a suggestive obligation, tending to sustain that attitude of confidence which is so necessary to successful prayer. The whole complex of the early Roman religion is eminently calculated to create just that habitual-mindedness which would have made of the Romans what they finally became, the most materially successful of ancient peoples.

The Greek practise was in detail very similar to the Roman, but had two or three distinctive psychological approaches. I am less sure of the working principle of Greek religion than of any other, since it was never, to the same extent as the Roman practise, incorporated into Christian use. What I make out if it is the abstraction of Principles of Activity, made into gods and goddesses in much the same manner as abstractions of physics, that is to say, of the behaviors of matter, were later made into laws. Thus Aphrodite is the active principle of sex attraction; Apollo, of the sort of illumination which accompanies musical and literary composition, identified with the properties of Light, Sunlight in particular. Mercury, who seems to have evolved out of a Trickster series, is the personalization of that odd trickster habit of the mind, the trickiness of fate, the swift and unpredictable flightiness of mind. In a way, one might say that, while early peoples made their gods out of complexes originating within themselves, the Greeks made theirs out of their observations of the way life works. They set them on Olympus, together and apart, whereas the Roman deities are usually found at home in the Things on which they worked. The Roman gods could be dealt with directly, as early Christians dealt with their Saints, who took the places of the Lares and Penates of pagan Rome. But in the gods of Olympus there is discernible that attitude of Olympian condescension, and the personal concern of Heaven for mankind, which later fulfilled itself in Christianity. How it works out in practise is this, that if a Greek woman longed for a husband, she prayed to the Cyprian Aphrodite; if a Roman woman, she paid assiduous attention to one of the titulary goddesses of the hearth and the home—essentials resident in all that the possession of a husband implied. If an early Christian woman wished to be married she invited the aid of St. Joseph, or the Virgin Mother, human beings who had attained to divine power in departments of life in which they were experienced—that is to say to the life principle underlying all that getting a husband involved.

What makes me sometimes suspect that I may not have mastered the Greek method is that I have less success with it than any other. But that may be in part because the details of the Greek psychological approach are less easily to be discovered in their religious remains.   Also I am aware of a faint resistance to Aphrodite and Apollo which is never present in my approach to the simple gods of the earth. If a modern woman wants a husband she gets him through her knowledge of his weaknesses, which is perhaps why she so often repents of her bargain.

Modern conditions afford no sort of opportunity to experience the religion of Egypt. Nothing of its psychological approach is available except what is incorporated in the *Book of the Dead,* all of which relates to the passage of the soul into the other life, and its conduct there. This is a pity, since the little we do know seems to indicate an empirical use of psychological knowledge which, after lapsing completely for a thousand years or so, has been modernly rediscovered. The cult of Osiris with its accompanying death rites, and otherworldness, lasted about four thousand years. During that time the Egyptians thought much of the life to come and invented methods for meeting every conceivable emergence of the discarnate soul. His objective was, first, to habituate himself to death, and then to reacquire gradually every one of the capacities of living, and, in all probability, the power of return at will.

The formulas for accomplishing these things are marvels of affirmative suggestion. They cover after-death necessities such as "Opening the mouth of Osiris," that is to say of the deceased posed as the god, or for "Not letting the heart of a man be taken from him in the other world," and another for restoring his memory to one who has been weighed in the balance of the gods and not found wanting. Here is the

key formula for the dying: "I am, I am.   I
live, I live, I grow and when I awake in peace
I shall not be in corruption."   And this is for
uniting the ghost to his god: "I have knit myself together, I am whole, my youth is renewed
within me.   I am Osiris the everlasting!"   This
is the method used by Jesus, identifying himself with the Holy Spirit by the affirmation of
such identity.   *I am the Way, the Truth and
the Life.*

There are also hints of mystical states in
which the neophyte attained "the Divine
Sense."   Use of the phrase the "divine ray"—
the god being prefigured as the sun—antici-
pates the idea of the Holy Ghost, a projection
of the personality of the god, made manifest
in his worshipers.   At the beginning of the
Christian era there had been for two or three
hundred years, communistic ascetic societies,
not unlike the Essenes, to which Jesus is believed to have belonged.   But perhaps the best
reason for supposing that the Egyptian system
of mystical approach was more advanced than
their religious remains witness, is the knowledge they seem to have had of the complex

structure of the soul, embodying so many ideas that science in every age finds itself coming back to again and again, as we shall later.

The Egyptians were undoubtedly influenced by India, with which they come in contact during the sixth century B.C., and claimed to have originated the most important cults and ceremonies of the Greeks.

Says a writer in the fourth century B.C.: "Keep this our sermon from translation, in order that such mighty mysteries may not come to the Greeks, and the disdainful speech of Greece, with its looseness and surface beauty, so to speak, take all the strength out of the solemn and the strong, the energetic speech of Names." This may be one of the reasons why I get so much less from Greek religion; the beauty of it is too much on the surface, too figurative, and there are none of those strong, those compelling words such as modern psychology has taught us can most easily evoke the latent powers of the subconscious.

Very little suited to my purpose came out of the Tibetan *Book of the Dead,* since it is not predicated on an acceptance of personal immortality, but merely on a conviction of ever-livingness, in which every turn of the wheel brings with it a new, a distinct personal identity. There is an Oriental belief that, as the soul progresses through its various reincarnations toward Buddhahood, recollection returns, and all its earthly lives lie clear in the Light. But from accepting this explicitness of reincarnation, some incontrovertible choice of my soul prevented. What interests me in the Tibetan procedure is its psychological likeness to the Egyptian; a long preparation by autosuggestion through and beyond the moment of death, amounting almost to hypnotism. It is difficult to see how a consciousness steeped in the Tibetan practise, if it survives the death of the body, could help being given its direction.

> While wandering along, separated from
> loving friends,
> When the vacuous, reflected body of my
> own mental idea dawns upon me,
> Grant that there shall be no fear, awe, or
> terror in the *Bardo*.

Entering into the Reality, undistractedly,
  listening, reflecting, meditating,
Carrying on to the path, knowledge of the
  true nature of appearances
May the Consciousness undistractedly be
  kept in its natural state.
When wandering alone separated from
  dear friends,
When the void forms of one's own
  thoughts are shining there,
May the Buddhas, exerting the force of
  their graces,
Cause not to come fear, awe and terror of
  the Transition,
When the five bright Wisdom-Lights are
  shining there
May recognition come without dread and
  without awe.

IX

ALL the foregoing is to explain how it happened that, confronted by an emergency requiring more than the available intelligence to surmount, I turned back to reconsider the grounds of an earlier search for that more than mortal aid which is always so close to man that it has been, and is still, the major subject of his imaginings. I began to look for the technique of survival where I had looked once for the technique of prayer, in the experienceable items of religion when religion was a matter of experience and not merely a subject of intellectual debate.

I looked with considerable confidence, because that first adventure had not been a disappointment. There is help to be had. There is more life in man than he has ever put to the proof. There is more power accessible than he has utilized. There is more knowledge in him than his systems of education take into account. And there is a body of experiential practise of which, if man has the wit to discard the explanations and adhere to the experience, he can easily avail himself.

I shan't go into the reasons why that body of traditional but freshly experienceable knowledge has been withdrawn from the common use, obscured by the dead leafage of belief. How completely it was withdrawn I discovered when I wrote something about my rediscovery of it for the editor of one of the avowedly most intellectual of our periodicals, a man supposedly trained by one of the most scholarly of our universities for that purpose. It was written before the new psychology had got very far with the new vocabulary, which may have had something to do with his telling me flatly that he didn't know what I was talking about. And that, I think, was very much the state of mind of the American Intelligentsia fifteen years ago—for all I can discover, it may be to-day.

Happily, however, the average man has never suffered such a breach with his past religious experience as has the professed Intellectual; he will not be so completely disconcerted at being asked to take that experience seriously as a possible index of reality.

In my search for the technique of the subjective approach to that Immaterial Reality,
intimations of which have always haunted the
soul of man, I had to conclude that Jesus could
not be studied as an average man, nor as an
intellectual. He was a genius; a genius whose
field was spiritual subjectivity; he was perhaps the greatest spiritual genius who ever
lived. It is characteristic of geniuses that they
arrive at their goal by methods that are so far
submerged in the deep-self that they are difficult to describe, almost impossible to communicate. Jesus arrived at the high spiritual
state described as "union with God"—he called
it "abiding in the Father"—as directly, as securely as the musical genius arrives at absolute
pitch. He struck into his own spiritual way
as easily as a man with an ear for music strikes
into a tune. And like all geniuses, he had difficulty often in getting past the lack of such
genius in his hearers. He would say to them,
"I have more to tell you, but you can not bear
it now." There is reason to believe that in
John, the beloved disciple, he found a more
receptive aptitude, which gives to the Gospel of

St. John its special value of the supposedly more intimate revelation. But in fact, the rest of his disciples were ordinary men who, if they could not plunge into the absolute pitch of their teacher's spiritual song, could presumably sing as taught, and devoutly wished to be so taught.

Jesus believed in the power of prayer. But aside from the note of his own practise in going apart "on a mountain" to pray, and his explicit use of affirmation as a mode of prayer, and his denial of the pertinence of inordinate public petition he left very little by way of personal technique. In the only formalized prayer model which he left the psychological progressions are:

Acknowledgment	Our Father ... in Heaven
Worship	Hallowed be Thy Name
Affirmation	Thy Kingdom come
Petition	Give us this day ... bread
Reaffirmation	Thine be the Power
Affirmation of ever-lastingness	For ever and ever ...
Affirmation of decision	Amen

This firm commitment of the intuitive and intellectual judgments to the content of the prayer is an important item in practically all formal prayer . . . Amen . . . Waiting happily upon fulfilment . . . May I be placed in a state of perfect Buddhahood . . .

Probably the manner of Jesus' own death, tortured and violent, prevented a public approach such as would have served as an example. Allowing the utmost to tradition, he expected for the repentant thief a release at once swift and secure, and saying *Father into Thy hands* . . . gave up the ghost. It was as easy as that for him at the last, therefore requiring no particular technique. But such a passage predicated a whole life spent in that state of consciousness which he called "abiding in the Father." The mystics among his later followers were so much at a loss for a technique which would enable them to maintain that state, that the chief objective of Medieval Christianity was to work it out with immense and heroic pains and much stumbling. More than half the ritual of the Church of Rome is the crystallized residue of that search.

The disciples of Jesus, besides being ordinary men, were Jews. There is no traditional mystical lore among the Jews except for those states which are emotionally induced. Something could be attained by going through agonies of depression—usually brought on by objective difficulties—repentance and abasement, followed by reactions of relief, recovered confidence and reversion to the evidence of history; but that was not much. To this day it is difficult to make a Jew understand that mysticism is of the subjective self rather than of the emotions. He leans to the belief that mystical revelation when rationalized is, by that process, caused to disappear out of existence. It is true St. Paul had intuitive flashes: that one about faith as the evidence of things not seen, and his notion of a "spiritual body" which seems to have been something like the "astral body" of the Orient, or the "animal soul" of Aristotle. He realized a meaning in the death of Jesus deeper than the fact, but he saw no deeper actually than the Jewish tradition of sacrifice.

All of which explains why the early Christian world was obliged to bolster up its own situation with spiritual practise salvaged from discarded "beliefs" of its pagan past. It was as a *belief* that Christianity maintained itself; its practise was eclectic.

This was the discovery that turned my study from the historic Jesus to the experienceable paganism that I knew.

Among the tribesmen, aside from the suggestive value of funerary rites, emphasizing the conviction of survival, the one death practise which had wide acceptance, was the death song, rising out of the conviction that survival is facilitated by meeting death in augmented states of consciousness. There is a universal belief that immediately after death, the soul can be helped on its way by offerings, and sympathetic holding in remembrance. So far as this is not merely an outgoing gesture of bereavement, it expresses a belief in an intermediate state in which earth-bound influences prevail over the spirit.

Among the Egyptians the favorable state in which to depart this life appears to have been induced by the assurance of having made all possible practical arrangements in advance. It was a state of intellectual confidence, toward which the whole of Egyptian culture contributed. The special emergencies of the after-life were anticipated by autosuggestive formulas of affirmation, combined with the identification of the soul with deific principles, as has been shown in an earlier chapter. These were carefully rehearsed before death, with the suggestion that they be used afterward, as emergencies were realized.

Among the Tibetan Buddhists, the whole religious life is a series of exercises in the control of consciousness. Some of these exercises are purely physical, such as fasting and the endurance of pain. Others are psychophysical, breathing, self-hypnotism and the like. More important are the purely psychic, an orderly progression of states of recollection, meditation, concentration, illumination. During these exercises there is continual autosuggestive stress on the idea that the faithful performance of the exercises will render easy the passage of the soul from one body to another.

As death approaches there is constant repetition in the ear of the dying, of the facilitating formulas, coupled with pressing on the arteries and other measures of actual hypnotic value. After death the recitation of formulas is kept up, preferably by a disciple or teacher, between whom and the dead there is already an established religious rapport.   The absent one is made the subject of methods similar to those employed by the professional hypnotist, when controlling his subject in his absence.

In Christianity at its most complicated, say from the eleventh to the end of the fifteenth century, there was prevailing intimacy with thoughts of death, accompanied by the assurance that survival was swift and certain.   The rite of Extreme Unction with strong suggestive value had been salvaged from its mid-Asian roots, related to incidents of the Last Supper, and given sacramental importance. The whole trend of Catholic thought was to stress the life of the other world as against this.   Saving rites were performed over the dead; burial in consecrated ground was practically obligatory. Communication after death was believed possible, but generally interdicted except in the form of miracles. One of the conditions of authentic sainthood is still the performance of miracles connected convincingly with the dead.

And from about the middle of the fourth century on, reaching its highest point about the beginning of the fifteenth, there was wide and often well directed experimentation in the movements of consciousness which make up the body of mysticism in all lands and ages. Evelyn Underhill, who has written competently and directly of Christian mysticism, declares that she can find no essential differences in the mystical systems of the Brahman, the Sufi and the Christian. Nor can I find any between these and the primitive religionists with which I am familiar. The differences and distinctions are in the explanations. The way of the mystic is the way of the deep-self of man, the way of inknowing, of instinct and intuition. Speaking modernly, it is the way revealed in the deeper levels of the subliminal self, or the highest reach of the supraliminal. The door to it lies so far beyond the reach of man's intelligence that it is only by long and severely conditioned effort that the individual can become conscious of activity within himself, and apply to it the criticism of a trained intelligence. It has been the serious handicap of mysticism in the past, that the intelligence to the threshold of which the mystic knowledge has been delivered, has been neither trained nor highly developed. I can find, no more than any other student, no distinctions of quality nor comparisons of more or less between what goes on in the subliminal self of a stone age Shaman and mystics like Jacoponi da Todi, St. John of the Cross, and Buddha himself. But in dealing with them, one has to be able to discriminate between the content and nature of the intelligences through which their revelations reach us. A stone age mystic has a stone age mind, innocent of logic and the scientific method, furnished only with stone age concepts of the universe and the nature of things.

X

It has been the weakness of Occidental man always to believe too much. It was the weakness of Christian mystics to limit their exploration of the inner consciousness by the tight but not restrictively narrow doctrines of a patristic and medieval Christianity. This gives to their interpretations often the effect of being narrower than they actually are. If, with a modern intelligence, you set about reexperiencing these doctrines, you discover that they are of a more extensive content than has been popularly believed.

Going back to the list of concepts and mental attitudes of our Occidental religious inheritance, we discover in the mystic approach certain essentials. First, we find "a clear conviction of a living God as a primary interest of consciousness; and of a personal self capable of communion with him."* It is not necessary, however, that the God envisaged should correspond in any particular to Jehovah.

*The Essentials of Mysticism. Evelyn Underhill. Dutton & Co.

The second essential to the successful practise of mysticism is a realization that it is impossible by intelligence alone to sort out man's various experiences of the universe and coördinate all their aspects with a felt reality. To reduce his experience to order, man must call into play all his higher and deeper subjectivity, and by intelligent criticism of his mystical activity, make a closer approach to the truth.

Starting with these essential motions of the mind, there is a considerable latitude of method, which may have its roots in the sex of the postulant, in his racial temperament, in his social environment, in his religious inheritance. The absolute test of the validity of a mystical experience is that it is a genuine motion of the mind. It is not essentially, nor inescapably, an *emotion,* although, in mobile temperaments, mystical experience may react emotionally in such a way as to over-fill the vessel of personality almost to the point of hysteria. One has to make these distinctions between the experience of mysticism and the individual reaction to its revelations. Especially one has to make them in respect to the technique of seeking and attaining such experience.

Very early in the history of man's discovery that by the motions of his psyche he could acquire knowledge important to his continued personal existence, he also discovered that every mystical state had a definite relation to at least two other states. All these states occur in an orderly sequence, one leading to another which may not be successfully reached without the first. When intertribal communication began, it was discovered that under whatever name these states were described, their consecutive order was the same, and that experience acquired in one tribal or racial mode matched with experience in every other. Medicine men could exchange experiences profitably, and methods invented or acquired by instruction became recognizable items of such exchange.

It was discovered, for example, that the first motion was to clear the self of prepossessing interests and emotions, to withdraw the least, remotest filament of attention from the not-self, in a state known as Recollection. Once this state of complete Detachment is attained, it is practised until it can be held without too much effort as Concentration. After this, at longer or shorter periods, according to the individual, normally occurs a state known as Dilation of Consciousness, in which the whole boundary of spiritual capacity moves outward to give the spirit room. From this point there is an orderly succession of other states of consciousness, culminating in complete Union with the Source; and this whole range of spiritual activities taken in their natural order, is known as the Mystic Way. It is traveled according to individual capacity and probably follows the same law of personal instrumentation that is observed in intellectual capacities.

In general, after one passes the first stage of the Mystic Way, in which detachment from the objective life is secured, it is important to realize that mystical technique is in every case *an activity of the subconscious,* phases of it taking place at deeper and deeper levels successively. In talking with the uninitiate, I often have the greatest difficulty in making them understand that mystical experience is not an activity of the intelligence, which only comes into play afterward to explain and verify the experience. Meditation, to a mystic, is not the same thing as "thinking things over," nor is Concentration merely the state of not thinking about anything else. Mystical revelation is the farthest remove from an intellectual conclusion.

So many good books are available on the technique of mysticism as variously practised, that it is only necessary here to note differences arising out of my stumbling into that Way, while engaged in a search which, although profoundly religious in its implications, had nothing to do with religious belief.

When I began seriously to walk in the Way of the Christian mystics, I believed little more about it than that the spiritual teaching of Jesus arose from a profounder spiritual insight than that of any other religious order. I knew by that time that much of the technique of the great modern mystics was rooted in the experience of the great pagan mystics, and trusted both of them the more for that. Spiritual experience, to be trusted, must be as universal as spirit. My experience with tribal mystics had taught me to discriminate between the universals of spiritual behavior, and the ways in which it expresses itself in individuals. And I had no sooner begun the discipline of Christian prayer than I discovered that it differed no whit from prayer among Amerind tribes, except that it was carried further and deeper. I found that I was already, from my years in the American desert, adept in the beginning phases of mystical technique, Meditation had become pleasant, the state known as Dilation, a habit instantly assumed. I had much help from the Saints in methods of Recollection, since the recollected spirit in the midst of modern life is quite another matter from the same state among tribesmen, where life is reduced to the bare bone of substance. Indeed, I discovered that the general cultural disposition of a period had much more to do with mystical proficiency than has been supposed. Also that habits of reading and ordered study such as are common to-day, greatly facilitate all the states of consciousness for which the de-

vout of the Middle Ages struggled unbeliev-
ably.

I had that easement which comes of being
born into a period when a university education
is a matter of course. And by the time this
specific study began, I had already written six
books, and had acquired reasonable practical
control of my own subconscious, in which I was
helped by such knowledge as was current in the
early part of this century.

One makes this explanation because of rather
general misapprehensions as to what one claims
in claiming mystical attainment: sanctity, superior moral practise, moral or intellectual infallibility. Because the great Christian mystics
applied their enlarged spiritual capacity to the
discernment of religious and moral problems
almost exclusively, it has come to be a common
interpretation that mystical gains can not, or
ought not, be counted in any other direction.
Having gone into it for the sake of discovering
how far, and in what way, subjective capacity
can be made to serve those exigencies of daily
life which lie beyond the reach of available objective help, I never attached any more sanc-

tity to my mystical proficiency than to that faculty for minute observation which enables me to study a flower blooming in the field and then go home and locate it as to genera and usually species, without the common necessity of plucking and pressing and pulling apart.

All of which leads on to saying that in the course of a few years I was reasonably successful with all the desired states; but that I never experienced a Vision. This might have had something to do with my having undertaken this practise without conventual and cloistered aid. I did not, as did the earlier mystics, rest all my satisfactions on mystical practise. This no doubt saved me from the intrusion of those illusory emotionalized states by which abused human nature recompenses its normal losses, such as become the acute problem of conventual life. At the same time it cut me off from some of the conventual achievements.

When I say that I had no Vision, I do not mean that my practise brought me none of that extended *vision,* the perception of reality beyond what the intelligence cognizes, of which it has been said that without it the people perish.

Nor do I mean to say that capacity for acute detailed visualization, which is so necessary to the creative writer, failed in any particular. It was, in fact, greatly augmented by mystical practise. One must distinguish carefully here, because in the United States there is a use of the word "vision" which I think does not obtain elsewhere. It has come to mean in the common speech, that type of executive visualization by which the high-powered salesman descries in advance how he can dispose of double his present number of porcelain bathtubs or copper-riveted overalls. A man of "vision" in these days is one who misses no tricks in planning a commercial campaign. In my youth it meant anybody who imagined sentimentalized alleviations of human misery through organized effort. When I use the word vision as the goal of mystical practise, I mean what the prophet meant: subjective perception of reality. But when I say Vision, I mean what the mystic meant in the middle centuries, a type of visualization in which the whole answering reach of mystical inquiry is gathered up and presented so vividly as to have all the force of actuality, and yet is understood as containing more than actuality, the sum and interpretation of actuality. To all the early mystics the Vision was the goal. The Way ended there as the Christian life ended at Heaven. For stone age mystics the Vision might be of the Great White Buffalo or the House of the Dawn; for Christian mystics it would be Christ in Judgment, God on his throne, Saints in glory, so disposed as to reveal in a moment of contemplation the whole divine mystery. There is always to the recipient of Vision, a sense of finality, of completeness, a cesura, if not the final closure of the Way.

And I had no Vision, because in my own approach I had had no sort of prepossession about the end of the Way. I traveled toward no Heaven nor anticipated any Hell. Unconsciously, my own thinking about consciousness had been colored by our scientific perception of activity as unending; a universe forming, reforming; motion and change without rest. Possibly the Vision, which seemed to have occurred less often, or not at all in the more intellectual mystics, marks the limit of individual capacity for extended experience.

The influence of the scientific mode of thought has been to teach men to live their intellectual life in an unbounded plain of discovery. To live the spiritual life in unbounded experience, of which the fruit is more experience and more spiritual, without appearing to arrive at any point of absolute equilibrium, appears to many people a much more difficult matter. Many a human spirit, able to conceive an infinite God, fails before the prospect of an infinite extension of experience with him. Or, perhaps, realizing intuitively the end of its individual capacity so to experience, envisions that limitation as a Happy Hunting-Ground or a Christian Heaven. But the loss, to minds still mystically inclined, of intellectual credibility in existing concepts of the Hereafter would naturally suggest that we are about to enter on new and uncharted extensions of the Way, in which death as a fact is not visualized as Heaven; in which the infinity of God is perceived rather than postulated, and infinity itself becomes experienceable.

Perhaps this explains why, though I subject all my experience of folkways to mystical meditation—after it has been subjected to intellectual meditation—folkways being my natural approach to the human spirit, I never have any Vision of the Hereafter. I never, in my mystical experience, *come up against any break, any pause even, in spiritual modes, which would indicate the place where, in our objective acquaintance with it, death must be supposed to be.* I have experienced the Presence of God, I have known what the Christian mystics call Illumination, I have had instants which I think must be what is described as Union. But nowhere have I found or felt the dark.

One recalls in this connection that in the folk tales of death, the person to whom it occurs does not know at first that it has happened at all.

XI

AMONG the secondary phenomena of death, there is a type of story increasing in frequency in all literatures, as we come down to modern times, relating to experiences undergone by the people affected by a death not their own. Indeed, one can scarcely sit down with any group of intimates without hearing of the incidents which give rise to them, related as true to the teller.

There will always be the sort of thing that gave rise to mediumship, considered as phenomena of survival; but by far the greater number, going back into the literature of the stone age, are tales of hauntings; hauntings of localities, usually the place of death; or of objects, usually the property of the dead or the death instrument; or hauntings of persons, particularly those who have given offense to the dead either before or after. There are tales of reappearances, of spirits that contrive to assume the counterfeit of life for a short time, revealing their true nature later. These are extremely common in primitive literature. Then there is the tale of the family ghost which establishes itself as a sort of family guardian, banshee or tutelary-genius; in which class belongs the ghost that reappears to point out the site of buried treasure, or missing documents, or for the purpose of righting a wrong. Much later there is the story of ghostly appearances which appear to have no special significance; the stories of rappings and table tippings and automatic writings upon which the modern psychic research is based. All these, in literature, are usually related in the person of the ghost, but for our purpose they can only be treated in the person of the recipient.

A story which is widely discovered among Amerind tribes, is the ghost-marriage, in which the leading character yields to an unexpected seduction, only to discover himself the next morning sleeping beside a skeleton. A favorite version is one in which the ghost-wife or husband persists in the attachment and follows the other party about, until ridded by incantation. This story undoubtedly belongs in the same class as the story of the dead wife, sought in the Other World, almost drawn back to life, and then lost by the untimely kiss.

In this group belongs the story also popular in tribal life, of the dead friend, who "comes for" one who is about to join him in the Hereafter. I have known several such instances among my Indian friends, and in one case the waiting "spirit" was seen by several other tribesmen. In one of the villages in which I lived, years ago, populated almost entirely by people of mixed Spanish-Indian blood, there was a woman who used often to see these ghostly visitants going into the houses, even when they were not seen by the persons for whom they "came." Also I knew an intelligent and sensitive Irishman who would never give up and admit the possible death of a friend or member of his family until he became aware of the waiting presences invisible to the rest of us. They were entirely real, to him, and had a definite spatial location.

Once I wrote a short story in which a man became aware of his dead friend *inside him* altering his whole view of life. Never had I so many personal responses to any story, so many letters relating an identical experience. I should like to have these experiences, which have occurred to me as often as to anybody, credibly explained. I should especially like to see, reconsidered in the light of modern psychology, the whole body of tales in which the dead are described as rendered unhappy and even impotent in the next life by the neglect on the part of the living of rites designed to assist and strengthen the departed. These are older than priests, much older than codified beliefs. As a folklorist, I am not satisfied with any current explanation, and this sort of thing can not be reduced to experienceable terms. It is not possible by any modern means to experience a ghost personally and at will. Said Winnenáp, the Shoshone Medicine Man, to me, "If the dead be truly dead, why should they still be walking in my heart?"

There are, of course, modern explanations which may be the true ones. Tales of hauntings may often be accounted for by sensitivities, commoner than we ordinarily think, by which the traces of events and personalities are left in localities or upon articles associated with them. The story of the ghost-marriage and of the dead wife or lover almost won back, and frustrated by a kiss, is, say the psychologists, a dream experience frustrated by waking. The story of the spirit appearing as a death warning has been explained as an intuitive prevision of death delivered at the level of conscious attention by the only means available—the means of visual hallucination.

What I wish to point out in this connection is that though these may be the true explanations of death tales, all of the incidents are precisely those which would be logical if death were actually found to be what primitive man believed it to be, a mere severance of the spirit and its instrument, the spirit going on unaltered, except for the loss of its instrument, in nature and constitution. It is not at all illogical to suppose that a spirit of not very advanced development, uninstructed about death, shocked by a violent and terrifying death occasion, might not continue to linger on, to "haunt" the spot of its demise indefinitely. It is entirely possible that when one has passed one's whole life believing that there can be no rest or release for the spirit without the performance of certain rites, one does not immediately surrender that belief on meeting the occasion of death. A discarnate spirit might truly fear to go on its way without the consoling rite.

Or suppose you died, firm in the conviction that your friend entertained a view of life detrimental to his welfare? Would not your concern be to get back to him with a last admonition? It is the extreme naturalism of most ghost-stories that makes it so difficult to accept an explanation arising in our own psyche, unprompted by any motion from the dead; especially when our own intellectual beliefs about death contradict such reaction on our own part. Why should one committed to the idea that death means simple extinction, experience, as we know he is as likely as ourselves to do, the sense expressed in saying, "My friend was never so near to me, we were never so completely reconciled."

I do not see how we can avoid taking these popular tales of death and the dead, into account as incidental phenomena. Still more must we consider the stories that grow out of the psychological experiences of death not our own. There is first, the shock of the wound of death; apart from the recurrent discovery of loss, the ache of the severed habit of association. It can occur, the shock, even when the death is looked upon as a blessed release for all concerned. The nature of that shock has never yet been explained psychologically. Grief one can understand, the long ache of absence. But why, if death is "natural" in the sense of being the inevitable decay of a self-conscious entity, the common lot of every such entity, should its occurrence in another a little before its occurrence in myself be so severe a lesion as to threaten, as we know it does, the life complex of the one who is left behind?

There are analogies to these things in nature which are not without suggestive value. The tree does not bleed for a dead leaf; but for a living branch torn green from its side, the tree itself suffers a wound, has often died. How much is sorrow, "the beautiful companion of immortality," the witness of a mutual pang? In the absence of all proof that the essential nature of spirit does alter unrecognizably, I do not see how we could get out of admitting that in all probability a surviving consciousness is subject to the same upsettings of grief, fear, joy, awe, the same struggles against and endeavors for conditions to be avoided or desired, that attach to it in this life.

As a folklorist I do not entirely discredit the explanations of the psychologist who maintains that all the secondary phenomena of death, even those that take place before the event, arise in our immediate emotional reactions; but neither can I deny the logic of the universal primitive belief that it is only the conditioning of consciousness that alters with death, and not its essential nature.

I have already explained why I give no place to the so-called "psychic phenomena" of mediumship, and only mention it again in connection with what seems to me a curious contradiction in our thinking about death, inasmuch as we profess a belief in a theological philosophy which assumes that in death there is no loss of the spiritual gains of living. And yet we approach the dead by a method which implies a complete regression into more primitive planes of consciousness. We accept, so far as the postulates of mediumship are concerned, lapses from the high intellectual plane upon which the "spirit control" has passed its term of livingness, that we would not tolerate under living circumstances.

I agree with other students of primitive life, that many states of consciousness (classed generally by the medical profession as hysterical, meaning, beyond their capacity to resolve) are easier for tribal man than for us. Automatism is easier, hypnosis, trance, probably death itself more accessible. But I can not discover in this circumstance ground for supposing that death reduces modern man and Dawn-man to the same status. Surely man's evolution into an intelligent ghost should not lag perceptibly beyond his normal rate of acquiring intelligence.

Why should the ghost of a Dawn-man— admitting ghosts to our category of realities— be any more like the ghost of a modern man than the intelligence of the Dawn-man and the modern man are alike? Why should not ghosts whose baggage of self-knowing intelligence and traditional knowledge was small, have been pale, timorous shapes, haunting the familiar places rather than the strange country of the Beyond? Why should they not have gibbered who had learned little else in life, why not discovered, in warning and advising the tribe, a more interesting occupation than was afforded by the type of discarnate life into the midst of which the spirit of the Dawn-man found itself suddenly projected? And on the other hand, why should modern man accept at the hands of his departed friends a communication at levels so far below those they have recently abandoned? There is a logic in the death lore of tribal man which is lacking from the lore of psychic research.

Unless——

Unless we go all the way with tribal man who never felt his own logic of life disturbed by the intrusion into it of occasional irreconcilable instances. The reader must go cautiously here. When I use the term Dawn-man, I mean explicitly early man now out of our reach except as his experiences have been preserved by tradition, or by inference of the stages of social evolution that must have been covered by him. When I say tribal man, I mean primitive man in the cultural state in which he is still accessible. Primitive, in my vocabulary, becomes a general term to cover cultural ranges between which and modern times there is the sharp dividing line of organized communication, through the invention of some means of writing, and organized mechanisms, such as go by the name of machines, mechanical instruments in which two or more mechanical principles are coordinated. And when I speak of tribal man I am drawing on experiential contacts with American Indians corrected by considerable book knowledge of other primitives. Chiefly I discover the qualitative differences between myself and tribal man to be intellectual rather than subjective and not always to my advantage. The cultural differences are more marked, but still not so pronounced as popular estimation supposes.

I recognize in myself the same psychic gestures as are found in tribal man, identical motions of consciousness in man and in the lower forms of life. But these gestures and motions are no longer qualitatively alike. In me, as distinguished from the Dawn-man, consciousness is instructed and informed by all it has experienced since the Dawn-time. There have been exchanges between my soul and the whole purpose and intent of consciousness. I am no longer, as the Dawn-man was, a complete stranger to my Source. The Son, through the knowledge of himself, has knowledge of the Father. Consciousness has undergone an evolution in respect to itself.

It has experiences within itself that can not be defined as intellectual and have no relation to the process known as thinking; intense activities that have been as important to its existence as objective experience has been to intellectuality. Grief has been one of those activities. Fear is one. Thinking intelligently about death is another.

Tribal man does not think much about death, but he experiences as much, perhaps more, since he has never inhibited any of his experience on the ground that it is "morbid," or contrary to accepted tribal notions about the constitution of the universe. Collecting the record of that experience and checking it against records of man everywhere in the world, I seem to discover not only all that has been already stated in previous chapters, but a little more of primary importance. Everywhere the idea of man as daunted by his experience of death, more or less frightened and perplexed by it, has prevailed. The more primitive man shows himself, the more anxious a moiety of his ghosts seem to have been to get back into this life which they have been forced to abandon; the more rights and exorcisms to which man has had to resort to persuade them to go away and stay away. Everywhere tribal man is discovered accepting what he esteems as veridical experience, which suggests that the desire to return is particularly insistent with the newly dead; and it is the newly dead who seem to exhibit most resentment at the change, amounting at times to active malice toward the undead.

Tribal man believes himself to have reciprocal access to the dead, affecting and being affected by them. The changes he thinks of as taking place in his dead, are subjective changes, the new powers acquired by them are subjective powers. In the majority of ghost-tales, these powers are precisely the *powers man seems to have been obliged to surrender on the road to complete intellectual rationalism.* Where loss of power, by death, is predicated, it is almost without exception loss of intelligence. Every tribe of my acquaintance has its tale of a poor befuddled ghost, a "crazy ghost," so disoriented by the catastrophe of death that it merely haunts and gibbers, unable to get itself together sufficiently to work a positive harm. Incidentally, tribal man presupposes the ghosts of all the higher animals, and never draws a sharp line of distinction between animals that may and may not survive recognizably.

The interesting item in all this, is that it is precisely the sort of ghostly behavior to be expected *if* survival is an evolutionary link in an ever-living chain. This is the way ghosts of men in states of unstable equilibrium between the major subjectivity of animals and minor intellectualization of primitive humans would behave. It would be part of our normal expectation that, as men understand themselves and their universe better, something of the habitual poise which is the purchase of such understanding, would pass with whatever it is that succeeds in passing the ordeal of death.

This brings me back, as so many of the turns of the road do, to a new consideration of mediumship as a possible bridge across to the country of the dead. What the most cursory inspection of the records of research by mediumship makes apparent is, that it is easier to reach inferior intelligences by this method. Or else that the only means superior intelligences have of reaching back, is by way of regressions which are practically worthless as a method of informing us of the actual condition of the dead. Or that superior intelligences, by the fact of their superiority, definitely renounce this means of communication.

Going back to tribal man, we find him communicating with his dead by means of fixations entertained both by the living and by the dead when they were alive. Primitive man knows very well that neither love nor sorrow will bring the dead back. He does seem to have believed, however, that by the use of suggestion, received before death, and through the subliminal activity of special types of persons, capable of regressions of which the trick has been long lost to the average, somewhere in the womb of consciousness the dead may be reached. If there was ever any logic in tribal man's lore of death, then the modern practise of mediumship omits the primary requisite for successful passage back to the level of intellectual cognizance. It is not the desire of the living to know nor the wish of the departed to communicate, that bridges the gap; it is the suggestion received by the subjective self *before* death which gives the clue to the backward-reaching soul. By all the logic of our present knowledge, what we should do is to impress on the living the *necessity* of their coming back; we should work on living souls the compulsion that the professional hypnotist contrives against his subject. From all we know of consciousness, there is a great deal more likelihood that the dead so impressed, especially near the time of departure, would find their way back, than that they should come in response to the willingness of tranced "mediums."

There would be a danger to be avoided; that of communicating to our own deep-selves a suggestion which would lead to subconscious mimicry of the dead which would delude our own intelligences. Nevertheless I should like to see such an experiment, predicated on what we know of the nature of consciousness, and its behavior under suggestion, tried out under intelligent conditioning. Again and again I have asked myself, why do we rest our answer to so important a question upon the pseudo-primitive regressions of secondary intelligences? Why do we not impress into the service of our inquiry true primitives and indisputable intelligences?

XII

I KEEP turning these secondary phenomena of death in my mind because of an obstinate prepossession about possible relationships between what the dead may be doing and what we do.

There may be no relation at all. Between man and his ghost the connection may be similar to that between the caterpillar and the butterfly, an interim in which the whole stuff of conscious personality is melted down to formless material out of which are forged new types of conscious creatures having no resemblance to what they were. This is entirely possible; but I don't believe it. The whole insect complex appears to me one of those explorations of blind alleys which life is occasionally found attempting. The caterpillar-butterfly experiment was tried a long time ago and never repeated. The superior and infinitely more complex stuff of which self-conscious individuals were fashioned, did not lend itself to melting down successfully. The almost purposive emergence of the self-cognizing instru-

ment as an evolutionary goal, does not carry
with it the necessity of an intermediate stage
of pupation in consciousness. If something
similar takes place in individual cases, it is more
likely to be a reversion to type, the working out
in remembered terms of an incidental suggestion.

The logic of life after death is, that life before death should constitute a preliminary
contributive stage of individual evolution.
Death as phenomena can not be an accident,
in the sense that the time of it, or the manner,
is accidental. The act of death, as we have
assumed for purposes of this confession, is an
inherent necessity. We pass from this phase
of existence to the next one because this phase
is inherently destructible. There is no evidence
whatever that life experimented in indestruc-
tibility; there is no sort of evolutionary logic
in the time-endurance of bodies. Or perhaps,
you might make out a sort of irregular progression, by which destructibility preponderates as
a characteristic of bodies endowed with the
highest types of consciousness. Death resistance in a sequoia tree exceeds by thousands of

years the same resistance in an Aristotle. It is not time but vitality of death-resistance which is important to the individual. Man's will to live is acute, on most occasions. But always we are confronted with this singular inconsistency that man, more than any other creature, appears to be subject to strange impulses to throw his life away. Among the important, and, for my purpose, unresolved secondary phenomena of death is War.

Nearly a score of years ago, anybody who looked upon this world from the perspective of another planet where such things are not done, would have seen millions of young men rushing on death with avidity. All the time it was going on, involved in it neither by participation, nor through the sympathetic magic of what is called patriotic emotion; that was how I saw it: a vast rushing upon death. Host upon host, overcoming the will to live by trumped-up emotions, by illicit traffic in tradition, by obligations not felt but pretentiously put forward against the natural resistance of life to extinction. I saw old men, impotent of such an act for their own part, flinging youth to the Devourer with passion, women braving themselves to sacrifice by the same motions as they braved themselves to childbed. So flimsy were the inducements that almost they failed to hold; almost life prevailed against the invitation to death. But not quite. Not until the impulse was slaked by exhaustion. Looked at by one to whom the intellectual and emotional reasons for doing anything are seldom found to be the primary reasons, that was how it looked.

That's an old trick of Consciousness. Man once ate his first born. Woman passed their children through the flame to Moloch; Aztec parents rejoiced if they saw their babies weeping on the way to the altar of sacrifice, since tears were a good omen. The further you go back the more you find life flung wastefully for the sustaining of life. Was it something the Dawn-man brought up with him out of the primordial slime, this notion that there was a need somewhere for life to be so nourished? Is there still a need that the great Unconscious should absorb back into itself that which it has given forth? Hath Death its own necessities? And are they dire to us, or benevolent?

It is not war that is trumped up; but the reasons for particular wars. What I ask myself is, what relevance has the need of war to this inquiry? There is a felt need. So much is it felt that wise men, men wise in the habits of the psyche, propose as a cure for war something *like* war in its psychological satisfactions; something that will do for the soul of man what war does. What then is that fruit of war on which the soul of man feeds? What but death! What other contingence is produced so completely and for such numbers?

There is a conflict apparent in man's individual approach to war which confuses the issue for those who look no deeper than the immediate life. The conflict is between the drive of the deep-self and the immediate self, between the deep-self and its instrument. Resistance to death is characteristic of all the instruments of life; but the soul is often biased toward death. Conflict in the emotional and intellectual life may deter from a particular war, but fear of death almost never. Far back in the life of tribal man, war figures as a possible release into the domain of death, *on a high level.* Contingencies of victory and of sudden death are both prepared for; both anticipated. Death rites are recited, death songs sung. That is what being "prepared for death" once meant, still means, religiously considered. It meant having your interior life raised to the highest possible plane of activity; it meant calling up to the appreciable surface of personality all the submerged strength of the soul. And that is what William James had in mind when he wrote of a substitute for war; something that would excite men to the highest possible states of consciousness. But it did not occur even to William James that death is the one item that does so for all men at almost all times, death faced by choice.

William James suggested voluntary poverty, which is near the mark. Poverty means mutilation, surrender of the fatness of life, and the sacrifice of things esteemed desirable, which has always been regarded by man as a normal gesture toward high states of consciousness. Men who have adopted a policy of peace, as in the Middle Ages men in monastic orders did in great numbers, have sacrificed their maleness along with riches and place, to attain the necessary high states; and the chief goal of monastic life has been, by and large, to make a good death. That is to say, to reach through death, by meeting it on a high plane, to a permanently high plane of ever-livingness.

So there is no way in which I can dissociate war in my mind from the other secondary phenomena of death; no way in which I can make a recommendation toward doing away with war until I have made some sort of resolution of our common problem of dying. Why should our old men mouth falsely, our women deny the purchase of their childbed pains, in order that our young men should be afforded an unprecedented opportunity to die in great numbers under cover of coveted states of consciousness? Is there not some color here of an urge deeper than all our arguing about it, so deep that we have no way of rationalizing it but the ways which our best intelligence refuses?

There is only one way I know of getting

at this disposition to die largely by war, which afflicts our most intellectual as well as our least intellectual societies.   It is to reexamine our lore of death in connection with the history of war as a social phenomena.   Possibly war is only popular by long association with high states of consciousness, and we throw ourselves into the one because it was once a favorite and easily accessible way to the other.

Once, on a hint given me by the Priest of the Bow at one of the Rio Grande pueblos, I wrote something about educating our ancestors. He said the trouble with the white man's efforts to educate the Indian was that they were all directed to the education of the particular Indian, they never reached to the ancestors which he carried about inside him.   We had a long talk about it; that was while the Great War was going on, and I mentioned to him this strange frenzy of rushing on death, which afflicted the world.   What I wished to know of him was whether the impulse to war was simply the ancestors working in man, struggling, in a time of particular spiritual depression, to raise the spiritual voltage by the only rite they knew.   He was explicitly of the opinion that what we should have worked on was the Main Stem of Consciousness.   Those were not his words, but a translation into my vocabulary of his figures of speech.   He thought if we worked at rites calculated to increase the *wakonda* (the essential energy) of humanity, war would not have happened to us; it happened he said, war and pestilence and other means of riddance, when the *wakonda* of the race was low, as game failed when the Master of Life for any reason failed to put forth that *wakonda* in life-forms.

I recall too, that he thought it might be because the white man never took pains to placate the souls of those he had slain by adopting them into his tribe.   He told me exactly how it was done and advised if it were omitted after *this* war, the sort of thing that has happened would happen.

That was how I came to write about educating our ancestors, because all that the Priest of the Bow said was to the effect that there is more to humanity than the little that is visible to the objective intelligence.   It was all predicated on the tribal conviction that consciousness is inherently indestructible, and that no limb of humanity, though apparently severed by death, is ever without its reciprocal effect upon the whole body of a self-cognizing race. Which seems to me the only logical conclusion about death and the dead that can be made from that premise. I have not studied these things sufficiently to know to what extent history corroborates the Priest of the Bow in assuming that war, as well as famine and pestilence, are more commonly experienced when the *wakonda,* the essential energy of consciousness, is low, whether from too much fatness, too great a fixation on the gratification of sense and the objective satisfactions, or too desperate a poverty of spiritual desire, or possibly, too great a proliferation of individual forms. I put forth this earlier concept since we have scarcely bettered it, for what it is worth, making sure I shall have your agreement thus far: that wars such as we have recently experienced, are unlikely to occur to peoples in a high state of spiritual consciousness.

Wakonda; orenda. I give you both words, both meaning the same thing, as indispensable additions to a vocabulary without which we shall not be able even to discuss these things intelligently. Both of them refer to the outgoing activities set up by alterations in the stream of consciousness passed through one or another instrument, or group of instruments; something analogous to the magnetic field occasioned by the passage of the electric fluid through iron; the *orenda* of Germans in a state of high interior activity over their group destiny, the *wakonda* of Americans in the throes of one of the periodic fluctuations of possessiveness, to which their economic constitution exposes them; the *orenda* set up by the sudden appearance on the windy Plains of the Hereafter of a million newly dead. Until we cease to treat death as a personal and private disaster, and realize to the full its social implications, we shall never know any more about it than the Priest of the Bow knew, and we shall continue to guess much less intelligently.

I was never able to sell what I wrote about educating our ancestors because nobody ever knew what I was talking about. No more do they when I talk so about war. But I can come to no conclusion which does not involve a question in my mind as to what happens to the parent consciousness, the stem of the race, in the event of such holocausts. If the end is nothingness, then must the wound of death be reciprocal, and consciousness expends itself infinitely without repayment. If livingness—supposing it a reality—exists at the heart of life, then extinction—if that is the reality—must lurk there also. One of these eventualities must be a constitutional factor of consciousness, informing all its behaviors. Of which of these is war the symptom?

XIII

THIS is what our traditional lore of death comes to; an attempt to ward off the menace of death by the motions of man's own mind. It is only within the last quarter of a century—popularly within the last decade—that we have been able to see it so. Without our modern knowledge of the relation of man's immediate intellectual self to his subjective selves, we should never have been able to translate the language of myth and poetry in which man's intercourse with the Great Mystery has always been couched, into the facts of subjective experience.

It is true we have not been able to go so far with the intellectual exploration of man's subjective perceptions, as is necessary for the complete rationalization of all its processes. We have but made a beginning, of which the whole significance seems to be that, as the emerging intelligence of man can more and more be trusted to deal with immediate and objective concerns of the life processes, the deep-self occupies itself with the aspects of those life processes which exceed the intellectual span. More and more, as intelligent man has learned to handle the objective realities of food and housing, reproduction and social responsibility, he has come to exercise a more enlightened supervision over the activities of his deep-self. He realizes at last that the hinterland of the mind is more extensive, more varied and possibly more important than the definitely bounded territory of the conscious intelligence. It is now fairly understood by all rational societies, that, in general, man's possibilities of maintaining himself as an evolutionary feature of the universe, depend on his successful mastery over, his intelligent use of, the country of the unconscious.

Physiological science, if it reveals anything of man's destiny, indicates that as a physical mechanism, man is past noon of his evolution. Although physical death is not actually known to be "natural," in the sense of being inherently unavoidable, in the absence of any single indisputable instance of escape, we have to treat it so. And, curiously, physiological science, without any premonition that it would turn out that way, is continually dredging up evidence of the extent, the importance and the historic continuity of subconscious life processes. What constitutes a man's Sacred Middle appears to be a series of excerpts subconsciously selected from his physical past. What holds a personality together, what sustains the mechanism of self-conscious intelligence, is a collocation of *sub*conscious processes by which tissues are built up and made to function, toward which the chief office of the intelligence is to protect it from outside attack. So protected, the subconscious entity seems to be able to manage its own business with remarkable competency.

Putting aside the question, at present unanswerable, as to whether the subconscious of individual man, which we have always naturally treated as an entity, is an entity evolved out of the life processes; whether it is an entity elsewhere evolved, taking up its residence in the life complex; or a force analogous to electricity, becoming involved with the life complex and proceeding to consolidate and shape an identity; we ask ourselves the question which most concerns us: What is its business? Can the business of this entity be guessed from what we know of it; can what we know of it throw any light on its business? What we have just been trying to find out is whether its business can be accomplished in the life span of the body. Or does evidence demand, or even intimate, the necessity for a continuing existence in another instrument?

We have just run over the history of man's early efforts to make something out of his intuitive perception of his own ever-livingness— what he took to be an ever-living quality, because, though he perceived that all animals die, he could find no evidence in his Middle that sustained this objective observation. We find him from the first concerned for the welfare of this ever-living part of himself, and at the same time depending upon what it could teach him for a method of fostering and securing its prerogatives. And we find him using—untaught by anything but experience—precisely the methods that our most advanced science indicates as the underlying procedure of what we call evolution, certainly the method from which most is hoped for in the further education of the spirit, the method of suggestion. We know more of the true inwardness of suggestion than did tribal man, and can explain it to our greater satisfaction. We can do more laboratory tricks with suggestion, but we make no use of it not anticipated by our remote ancestry.

I have tried to indicate, as briefly as possible, the folklore way of separating these items of man's primitive use of his subconscious part, but I undertake no responsibility for convincing anybody. Whole libraries of the lore of tribal man are available for the inquiring mind. There are also, among the six continents, four, in which the workings of the tribal subconscious may be experimentally studied. In every case, the challenge is from the writer to the reader, and his the responsibility for not knowing what is important to be known. My own private conviction is that, except, perhaps, in the field of psychotherapeutics, modern science has not yet overtaken the subjective practise of the medicine man.

By all our intellectual gains over tribal man

we are bound to value his intuitive perceptions about the nature of his inner self *in proportion as they are intuitive and unrationalized.* We are bound to consideration for the primary, intellectually untutored motions of the Dawnman's soul, by our commitment to the scheme of evolution, which employs, and proceeds by, precisely such processes. We can discard the earliest motions of man's intelligence as we do a child's, but if subconscious activity were capable of being completely mistaken, evolution could not be begun, man could not have emerged from his matrix of animality.

The first step then, toward a rational understanding of death, is to verify and reinterpret every item of man's subjective attitude about it. And that includes for its next step, a re-experiencing, in the light of modern psychology, of the Mystic Way.

I do not mean here to credit too much to the new psychology. I am far from accepting all the postulates of psychoanalysts, especially of the Freudian school, and have chosen in my own writing on these subjects so to express what I have gleaned from primitive contacts and otherwise, that the absolute vocabulary,

when it arrives, can be substituted for the words
I have used.   But I cheerfully concede that
modern psychology has given us a method, and
a vocabulary in which for the present, subjective experience can be intelligently discussed.

For our modern neglect of the Mystic Way,
I make certain allowances.   The whole modern
world has been too recently hatched out of the
superstition of belief not to carry a chip of that
eggshell yet on its shoulders.   It is possible
to find orthodox scientists—though not the
greatest ones—who fail to realize that a scientific conclusion is not a pronouncement from on
High, but a tool, which may make a breach
in our encompassing ignorance, and may, on
the other hand, crumple and dissolve at a
stroke.   And there are perhaps as many
shouters for the infallibility of Freud and Einstein as there ever were for the Pope or John
Wesley.

There is a notion among professional intellectuals that the business of the true scientist
is to inhibit intuition, and rest his conclusions
wholly on measurable evidence; but the very
great ones are discovered making use of their

own subjectivity as well as all other faculties, even admitting it in public. What has
kept them from unstinted use of the evidences of mysticism, has been the persisting
odor of sanctity which clings to every mention
of those orderly progressions of consciousness
by which the intuitive nature is enlarged to
keep pace with the extension of that intelligence which it is the business of all our educa-
tive science to foster. And on the other hand,
one finds men capable of knowing better, who
reject mystical behavior through sheer ignorance of how it works. I recall one who insisted
on leaving out Gautama Buddha from the
world's illuminati on the argument that, since
the prophet left home to follow his soul's quest,
he was "abnormal." But as a matter of fact,
continence, celibacy, are man's most usual gestures in the face of dominant spiritual enter-
prises, even men who, like the Buddha, do not
find it necessary to rid themselves of the demands of two hundred and fifty concubines.

Twenty years ago, when I wanted desper-
ately to find trained intelligences with whom
I could discuss my experiments in prayer, I

was always being disappointed in men of reputation, unable to accept that I could experiment in "Catholic" methods without being a "papist," or that I could arrive at effective prayer without the emotional attitudes of reverence and moral abasement with which it has been traditionally surrounded. Here in the United States the youth of our learned men has been so generally obsessed with the Protestant idea of prayer as emotional petition directed to a Source which you have first to "believe," that they simply can not grasp the idea of reversing the process and finding out by prayer, meditation, contemplation and other exercises, what there is at the end of that road which is worthy of reverence and inspires humility. In all my study, however, I found but one modern Protestant minister who had written informingly and studiously of prayer.*

I do not go so far as to say that explicit religious belief is a handicap on the Mystic Way. What I am disposed to think after long-continued detailed experiment, is that the association of particular religious beliefs with

*Harry Emerson Fosdick: *The Meaning of Prayer.*

the religions that have specialized in mysticism, is what has prevented our making the utmost practical use of the discoveries so made. If you believe, as the Oriental mystics do, that the main purpose of life is to attain such states of consciousness as will enable you to be completely absorbed into the mystery itself, you will not tend to develop your mystical faculties for any other purpose. If you believe with the Occidental mystics, that the main purpose of religion is to enable you to attain such states of consciousness as will produce the limited variety of "good works" included in the Christian category, in order that you may enjoy an eternal conscious ecstasy in the presence of your God, you will not strive for anything outside of that. But if you undertake the Mystic Way as I did, with the idea that it is one way of discovering what *is* at the heart of the mystery, and something of how it works, that is what you will get.

Not all at once and completely. The universe is not to be swallowed and digested in a lump. You follow the Mystic Way until you get beyond your experience; and then a little further until you reach the limitation of your intelligence to interpret, and there you stick. Always it must be borne in mind how new the intelligence is, how immature. Always it is possible to outguess, outsee and outfeel your intelligence. But you are bound to make a mess of trying to explain experiences beyond its capacity. Look at Swedenborg! Look at Mary Baker Eddy!

Another source of the general neglect of mysticism, is the failure to realize it as still going on among us. It goes on in conventual life less anguishedly, less dramatically than formerly, simply because of the longer experience behind it. The daily use of the Roman Catholic Church, and no less Catholic Anglican Church, proceeds largely by crystallizations of mystical discoveries into literary, but not too intellectual forms. Pick up any prayer-book of a long established, deeply experienced religion, and by perspicaciously omitting the passages that refer to explicit *beliefs,* or translating them into terms of your own beliefs, you discover that such beliefs are built upon the best-known principles of autosuggestion.

Examine, if you have the patience for it, half a dozen of the systems for acquiring mental power, extending your personality, reforming your character, such as preempt the first pages of the popular magazine advertising sections, and you will discover under them the easiest steps of the way, reduced to terms that flatter the prevailing American belief that any fool can do anything if somebody only teaches him the trick.

Few people appear to realize that non-Catholics may avail themselves of the privileges of "retreat," temporary retirement to monastic or conventual institutions in which are provided the necessary withdrawal and the favoring environment for the meditative life. But in fact few people realize that in the Old World such opportunities have always been available to those wise and intelligent enough to use them. When I live in London or New York, I make a retreat yearly, but here where the cloistering of the desert is always at hand, it is not necessary. If I seek the society of professional mystics now, it is chiefly to enjoy the exchange of experiences which, unhappily, are too rare to intellectual America—perhaps that's why its habitués complain about it so bitterly—and reimmerse myself in the intimate life of the spirit, the familiar talk about it, the inspiriting argument. It is still possible, if you know where to look for them, to find men trained in the spiritual exercises of Ignatius Loyola— the Jesuits will always give you the best argument for your pains—and if nothing else offers, there are always the psychoanalysts.

The genuine pursuit of that Way is a direct approach to immaterial reality. What we study is the behavior of essential consciousness. We begin at the threshold, disentangling consciousness itself from all that enmeshes it within the human complex, in somewhat the same fashion that the student of electricity separates the essential fluid from the phenomena it gives rise to. We do this largely by getting inside the phenomena experientially. We shuck off layer after layer of our immediate humanness, and pose that portion of consciousness over which we have control, in the attitudes arising successively out of other poses from which we have already extracted the meaning. We make the discovery that has been made by mystics the world over, that these poses have a causal relation, one to the other, that they are "normal" to consciousness and to each other.

After a while the experimenter arrives at what, to his own intelligence, appears a rational guess at the nature of the thing that is studied. We call it Buddha, Holy Ghost, or—this is my guess—the essential activity of Immaterial Reality. And this is where we all come out, Sufi, Buddhist, Christian, Mohammedan, Medicine Man; facing an Immaterial Reality, dealing with it, taking its measure. The Mystic Way is the only way man has ever invented for dealing directly with Immaterial Reality. Which is the reason why I feel sure that it is one of the ways in which we shall yet make sure discoveries about death. By it we approach so much closer to Immaterial Reality than we have yet been able to go with our intelligence, that we may eventually discover to what extent the soul of man is itself part of the Reality, partaker of its eternal quality.

So far, all the great mystics report their conviction of the ultimate union of the human particle with the essential Reality. They differ only as to the degree of separateness, of individuality it retains.

And that, in brief, is the mode of mysticism: a gymnastic of the inner self by which the source of that self is approached. The only belief that is indispensable to the undertaking, is that it will be worth the pains. The impression of cryptic utterance which is made by the works of the Christian mystics on the modern mind, is largely due to the limited vocabulary of Christian doctrine which is all they permit themselves. Not only the theological implications, but the phases, the imagery, the symbolism are all medieval and slightly fantastic to the modern mind. But when the teachings of the greatest mystics are translated into modern terms, you will find them highly provocative. And you needn't worry about the emotions; you won't be able to help having them, and they will be commensurate with your personal capacity. If you really wish, however, to push on to the extent of your capacity, it is advisable not to let emotion overwhelm you too early on the way. If emotion is what you are looking for, you won't go far to find it.

There isn't any end. You may arrive at a predetermined mark, which contents you, and there rest. Mine, for the early stages of the journey, was to discover what, if anything, answers prayer, and how it can best be persuaded. I found out so much more than I can ever find anybody able to talk over with me, that of late years, the search has rather lagged with me. But this is the point from which we must go on to discover why consciousness generally seems not to be aware of any such thing as death.

XIV

THERE is another, practically universal manifestation of subconscious activity, utterly ignored in this connection, which all unnoticed has entered into all our ideas of the way of consciousness in man. I have never interrogated the workings of genius for news of the soul's Hereafter, but other people are constantly doing it, and founding upon it a belief not only of survival, but all their concepts of the mode of life in a Hereafter so revealed. Several years ago I wrote a book on every man's genius* in which were set down along with observations on the method of genius, the conclusions drawn from such of the phenomena of mediumship as seemed to me to have been confused with psychological activity distinctly of the genius type. I must go back a little to bring the whole subject within the scope of this present inquiry.

From the earliest we know of man, we find him accepting a type of wisdom welling up

*Everyman's Genius. Bobbs-Merrill Company.

from within, especially after meditation or spiritual exercises directed toward creating a special flow of this inner knowledge; or, being called upon in desperate emergencies, is found rushing to his aid. No tribe is without this inner aid, and great men like Socrates and the Apostle Paul have confessed to trusting to its promptings. Christians called it the Holy Spirit, primitives named it the Ancestral Spirits, but in general, it gradually came to be called after the Greek idea of a special, individual spirit known as a genius. From the nature of the emergencies dealt with by genius, and its generally racial and yet universally human character, genius has come at last to be understood as a kind of wisdom, a knowledge of how to do things of personal importance and strongly marked ancestral characteristics, occurring in some degree in all men, but especially pronounced in individuals.

Under all the alterations of belief about genius, all the attempts to explain its origins as coming from inside or outside, gods or devils, the extent to which it is, or is not, amenable to direction by the person to whom it occurs, the one association it has never lost is with ancestral spirits. To this day the tribesman, confronted with a thoughtful emergency, will say, "I must go and talk to my fathers," meaning that he must go apart and in silence invite the prompting of his ancestral genius. And in this day it is generally conceded by those psychologists who have given study to it, that genius is the spontaneous play of ancestrally acquired aptitudes into the immediate life of the living generation. Whatever has been done by the genetically related group, *experientially,* over and over so that the gesture of doing has become part of the constitutional rhythm, a kind of dance of all the organic functions entering into that doing, that thing becomes more easily danced and done in the racial pattern. The technique of such doing comes to hand readily, requires less schooling, has been known to occur with such sharp definition as to be able to school itself without other tuition, to perfection in method, is, in fact, spoken of as "genius." Thus a Negro, an Aztec, a Jew, a Japanese will each express himself, even when brought up under alien influences and environment, with something inescapably ancestral.

All this is so well understood and so generally accepted that it would not be necessary to mention it, except for a way of speaking which we have fallen into, which denies, or at the very least, ignores the characteristics of genius in general. Among English-speaking peoples there is a fashion of not noting or naming as genius any but the supreme examples. Among these people, to call a man a genius means not only that he has genius, but that he possesses along with it noteworthy talent, and a high type of intelligence for handling it. So it is that the word has come to have quite different meanings according to the descriptive term which follows the classification. We say: that man has a genius for blacksmithing—or training horses, or cooking or whatever—meaning that he has known how to do these things without being directly instructed. But when we say: that man is a genius, we mean something involving our own reactions to the man, which makes it a breach of modesty for him to claim genius for himself. In other words, we have decked out genius in the exceptional degree with the tinsel of intellectual snobbishness, so that it is as difficult to discuss one's own genius frankly as to discuss one's own mystical experience without offense to the sentiments of sanctity which traditionally attach to it.

And yet, without such discussion, it is difficult to deal with modern aspects of psychic research honestly and scientifically. I have already said that in the case of Mrs. Curran, whom I have regarded as representing one of the most interesting, and neglected, types of subconscious activity, I could discover nothing that I could not have matched out of my own experience or that of my literary contemporaries. I still insist that I can sit down with a deck of playing cards or a bowl of clear water, and match subjective veracities of the unseen and the unknown with any medium I have been so far able to study, and do it without going outside the type of daily activities of the creative writer.

I have just read with interest the report of the mediumistic interview of Harry Price with

Conan Doyle. I admit in it a convincingness usually absent from such reports. And at the same time I feel certain that if Sinclair Lewis sat down to compose such an interview he could make it even more convincing with no more than his usual genius equipment. Nor do I feel that the fact that the medium employed by Mr. Price went into a somnambulistic state and delivered the interview in a voice and accent quite unlike her own natural speech adds anything to its evidential quality. The creative writer has also to go into a broody state, not quite trance because he must keep his intelligence awake, to criticize what comes through, in accordance with the literary standards he has set for his work. As in the case of Mrs. Curran, the only distinction I discover between mediumistic recreation of the personality of the departed, and the literary artist's recreation, is that the medium fails to apply to the work as it issues from her mouth the criteria of literary composition. What we seem to have in the medium—admitting honesty of intention—is activity which is wholly unconscious, as against, in the creative artist, activity that is guided and controlled by conscious intelligence.

What the successful creative writer knows about his own subconscious activity is, that he must watch over it, but not watch too closely. He must feed it with experience. That does not always mean that he must do in his person what his characters are expected to do, but that he can by successful psychological mimicry, by posing himself in the characters of his heroes and villains, by an intellectually directed form of sympathetic magic, acquire knowledge of the true inwardness of types of human experience in which he has not otherwise participated. I am quite sure that there are many American novelists of my acquaintance who could by this method "put on" the character of Conan Doyle with extraordinary verisimilitude. If the creative writer had in his head fairly complete information about Sir Arthur, and if he followed the usual practise of successful writers of pulling up his material from time to time, matching it up with his information, and pushing it back below the threshold where items of that sort are most effectively combined, I am sure he could present the absent personality far more convincingly than most mediums.

One of the items most frequently offered as attesting the supernormal powers of mediums, is information about the deceased that could not possibly be normally acquired. But that, too, is a thing that happens to creative writers; ask any of them. Moreover, there is a type of activity not infrequently found among geniuses—possibly one of the indispensable conditions of notable genius—which seems to be ignored among psychic researchers. That is the faculty of subconscious observation, observation of facts so subtle, so slightly objectified, that the observer himself is not aware of how information gets to him. Of this the late Luther Burbank is the most striking example I have personally known; although there lives to-day, not more than two days' journey from my home, a Navajo Indian who accomplishes wonders in the way of thief tracking, recovery of strayed stock and lost children by methods which I suspect are similar to Mr. Burbank's, in selecting out of three thousand hybridized seedlings the three best suited to his purpose.

In *Everyman's Genius* I have said all this, and more, to the effect that I can find no convincing distinction between the types of subjective activity in mediums and in creative artists, and no differences in their method other than those noted between conscious and unconscious control. What a literary genius could do in the way of overpassing the boundary between personalities still enmeshed in bodies, and those freed by death, I do not know, because it has never been seriously tried. Writers of reputation like Sir Arthur Conan Doyle, have been convinced by mediums or by mediumistic experience of their own; but I have had such experiences without being convinced in any degree.

What is true for me in respect to the phenomena of mediumship, is true of the experiences of the Mystic Way. The approach is different, and there is a difference in what one brings back, but there is no difference in the essential motions of the mind involved in the preparation for successful prayer and successful novel writing. There are distinctions in the effect on your character and the effect on your after-life, but none in the psychological mechanisms required in meditation, whether upon the Immaculate Conception or upon the Quantum Theory.

Detachment, recollection, concentration, meditation, the exercise known as dilation, are the same whether exercised in the interest of the Unitive Life, or in the interest of Black Magic—I am reminded that that is one sort of psychological experience I have not attempted.—Perhaps the method of the Unitive life, the gestures by which it is accomplished, are not found to differ greatly whether one is united with God or the Devil, though in the latter case one supposes attainment is quicker. I have already explained that when I finally reached Rome and could check up methods with orthodox mysticism, I found myself already advanced in the way, through having experienced primitive religion sincerely. What I discovered was that the various sorts of rewards and consolations asked for by prayer, required each its own technique. But these all kept toward each other a progressive relation, and it took me years to arrive at the place where I could certainly select in advance the method best to be used in particular emergencies.

But the same thing is true of literary technique. If you are a novelist with an idea you think would be better expressed in a play than in a novel, you can't just sit down and demand a drama of your subconscious offhand. You can't acquire a literary technique without being profoundly interested and in need of it, any more than you can pray for what you don't want. Neither can you arrive at any station on the Mystic Way which it is beyond your spiritual capacity to desire. Brother Lawrence arrived at the Practise of the Presence of God in the same way as the child Mozart arrived at playing on the clavichord—or was it the organ?—by a stroke of genius, without suffering a conscious struggle toward the desired end. Mozart had, in addition to musical genius, musical intelligence, and learned all that was necessary to communicate his genius to other men. But Francis Grierson, although he could compose amazingly, never could manage the approaches to genius so as to set down his compositions in intelligible form. Neither did the

French peasant girl to whom occurred the Vision of St. Catherine and Saint Michael, ever make any progress in theology, nor organize a spiritual practise in her own name.

Once, when I was trying to experience the passion of expiation that informs the brotherhood known as *Los Hermanos Penitentes,* on the *Rastre de Sangre*—the Trail of the Blood—that goes from the *Morada* of The Assumption, I think it is called, toward Pueblo Mountain, I experienced what is known as a Colloquy. I had gone all through Lent, to within about ten days of the Passion, without the whippings, of course, and without any expectation of crucifixion, which in any case would be denied to a woman. That I had made that passage with more success than I had expected, was, I thought, in part due to my intimate understanding of that mixed Indian and Spanish strain which can make of expiation a community exercise. I was doing the Stations of the Cross, at that late evening hour which is most favorable to the emergence of the subconscious, and I had come to the last station before the Calvario, which, because the ground is level there, is raised on a little pyramid of stones. As the light was, the cross, which happened to be large and of absolute proportions, stood up silverly.

I should say here that I am more sensitive to proportion than to any characteristic of form, and especially sensitive to gesture. So as I turned in the Trail of the Blood toward its lifted arms, I could no more help lifting my own with an outstretched motion than I could help what happened in the very instant that I found myself in the midst of Colloquy.

A Colloquy is a type of mystical incident in which there is a momentary splitting of the facets of the deep-self between which interchanges take place in the form of dialogue, as it might be between Soul and Sense, or between Soul and Saint or Soul and Savior. There are many such to be found in the writings of professed mystics, some of them of high literary excellence—I think of Mathilde of Magdeburg for example. It is ordinarily very difficult for me to accomplish these disjunctions; I can not even do automatic writing, except for a few moments as a *tour de force,* and this was only the second time in my life when one had occurred to me. But there I was in a pale ring of diffused light, such as encompasses a dream, holding discourse between myself, *as* myself, and Another, not visualized, but inwardly perceived within the shadow of the experience. What we discussed was the nature of the group-soul, and the things that might be affected through and by it, provided the group-soul could get such intelligent control of itself as is possible to individual souls. And at the end there was an extraordinarily illuminating passage in which the composition of the group-soul and its advanced activities were explained to me in language which does not exist. At the last instant the Figure turned, in a flash, an instantaneous glint of visualization; and I knew its Name.

Now I could account rationally for practically all but one item of this experience. It was inevitable that if I got any revelation out of my *Penitente* experience, that it would refer to the group-life. It would be practically impossible for me to work up any passionate sense of personal guilt toward the death of Jesus, in fact I hadn't tried. I had rested my personal approach on the common guilt of mankind, and especially American kind, in its rejection of the Spirit. And I had been trying, as much as I might, to get inside the group-mindedness of Spanish-speaking New Mexicans, which presents some interesting and unique features of group-amalgamation. Then I had been spiritedly discussing the matter of group-psychology with my hostess for this particular adventure, who had taken an Indian husband and advised me to do likewise, insisting that I couldn't know Indians, really *know* them, until I had known one in the most intimate relation. And I had answered back that every Indian was so deeply involved in his tribe that you never could know *one* until you had known the group.

That accounts for the subject of my Colloquy. That the whole affair transpired in the first Lent after the end of the war, and that my hostess and I had had many talks on the need of acquiring some way of raising the plane of group-thinking and feeling, since all we practise about it in mobs and panics and war psychology generally, accomplishes only regressions into lower forms of group-association, as in the herd and the flock and the swarm. That accounts for the dialogue form and the revelation of group-psychology which transcended my own capacity. I could even account for the face that in the last instant was turned toward me with a tender, but amused and slightly ironical twinkle. I knew it very well for my final choice, when I was writing my book about Jesus, and hesitated between the second-century likenesses, the face short, wide between the eyes and full above the ears, and the other long, high-nosed type with arched skull and forehead high without being narrow, the face of the Holy Coat of Treves.

You see why I have been at such length to recount this in detail; because the more detail the more easily you can realize that my Colloquy differed not at all in conception from the manner in which a story or a poem gets itself together in the mind of a writer. And it differed in actuality from a story, only in one essential and one small particular of time. It seemed to me to last a long time, since in the course of the Colloquy all that I had been able to collect by any manner of means whatever, about the group-psychology of animals, was reviewed and set in order around a new concept of the group as a psychological entity. When I undertook to write it out later, I was three months at it. But Mabel, my hostess, who was watching from an upper window, said that she saw me standing there with my arms outstretched not longer than the space of a *Pater Noster.* And I don't get whole books in as short a space as that ordinarily.

The essential in which this experience differed from other literary conceptions, was that when I tried to explain to other people the new light that I had on group-mindedness, and the way in which it could be utilized for social advance, I couldn't remember any of the words. I recalled the astonishing flood of items of information as to the way society is shaped among inferior animal groups, and the extraordinarily clear light on the central idea—hitherto unthought of—around which they grouped themselves. But I had no words in which to express the method of arriving at a higher type of group-consciousness. I am as certain as I was at the first moment, that I still know what I had been told, but I couldn't tell it. Years afterward, when Mabel had been more intimately received into her husband's tribal life, talking to me about the way in which *one* Indian became a constituting particle of group-consciousness, she said, "You were right. I know so much more about the tribal consciousness than I can tell you."

And that is my position to-day. I know so much more about group-mindedness than I can tell you. I know it. And the way I know that this is not an illusion is that I have made a little progress in twelve years in getting what I know to other people. What I lack is the descriptive vocabulary. I feel sure that if I could talk to anybody who had gone as far as I have in that direction, anybody who had worked out even one word or phrase of a vocabulary in which advanced states of group-mindedness could be discussed, that it would unlock for me the sealed revelation. For this, I am convinced, is the only way in which the

Mystic Way carries us beyond the reach of genius. I can't see any difference whatever in the method and the mechanism. Genius is what I said it is, the capacity to utilize freshly the experience of the ancestors; it is tied by its umbilical cord of experienceability to the matrix of the past of consciousness. Individual consciousness can go so far at the end of that tether as to be able to prophesy of the future; it can anticipate, but it can not actually experience the future.

All the great mystics admit that, by pursuing the Way, consciousness can know what is so completely unknown as to be untellable. Telling involves two factors, teller and hearer, and nobody can hear an absolutely new thing. The invention of vocabularies does not proceed in advance of experience; vocabularies really aren't invented, they are produced out of the communicable past, as leafage on a tree, to bud, flourish and fall with its growth. So there my book stands until the group provides me a medium of verbal communication out of new type of group-experience.

That was what happened to the mystics of old. They came at the end of the Way to a place they couldn't talk about, could only know and not apprehend. There is no certainty in the world like this. It is the kind of certainty you might conceivably get by being united momentarily with the Source of All Knowledge. Genius acts on that certainty in its little field, prophets die for it. It is probable that they would not so often die nor so cruelly, if they were more successful at explaining it.

This is probably what the great mystics meant by the Unitive Life. They are for an instant immersed in the Stream of Consciousness, immersed in its certainties. That was how I stood toward the group-consciousness of men, and so, of course, I know all about it even if I am instantly dropped back to a plane in which I no longer possess my knowledge. But if I could get back to it again with two or three others—— (. . . *Two or three met together in my name!*)

What I think noteworthy in respect to this experience, is that although it identifies itself up to the last moment, with the genius method, it passed over instantly without sensible dislocation into the method of mysticism. William Blake is the best example I think of in whom the genius method and the mystic method alternated and supplemented each other, like Browning's star, dartling blue and red without intermission. I believe that the identification of the two methods is one of the most important contributions that can be made to modern psychology. It enormously increases the number of individuals who can make a rational approach to Immaterial Reality, since the discipline of genius is to make that approach in full possession and keen exercise of conscious intelligence.

I think it would largely do away with my reluctance to a general dependence on mediums for exploration of the country of the dead, if it were known that the medium's necessary putting aside of his own immediate self had been acquired by the mystic method, so that he is enabled to retain his own intelligence. As this sort of research is now conducted, the medium, by some sort of self-hypnosis, puts his intelligence out of business temporarily. He can then with perfect honesty, since he is exercising no supervision over his subservient under-self, by means of the usual, wisely distributed genius method, construct something so nearly like a living picture of the dead, precisely as a novelist does it, that even his intimates could be deceived. I should be immensely interested in a medium sufficiently trained in the psychology of the unconscious to avoid its pitfalls, who with the eyes of his intelligence open would go along the immemorial way of the spirit toward the gate of death, and bring us news of it.

There are several inveterate items in the general mind which will render such an adventure unlikely for a generation or two. One of them is the innate human love of mystery mongering, which makes trance and other pathological incidents more interesting than the open way of the intelligence. Another is the wide-spread reluctance on the part of the masses who have lost their inheritance of genius, to admit the existence of such a faculty in the few. The possession of genius identifies a man as outstanding favorably among his contemporaries.

The gesture of mediumship is merely queer, and touched with the incitement of the interdicted. Genius is just the plain difference between one man and another, mediumship has popular connotations of magic and the miraculous.

Finally there is the sour residue of religious prejudice against the treasures of mystical attainment locked up in the Roman Catholic practise. Nobody has ever thought of interrogating the doctrine of the Communion of the Saints for possible traces of veracity on the lore of death. Once when I was discussing with a man whom Theodore Roosevelt introduced to me as "the most scholarly priest in America," the way in which the Confessional had anticipated psychoanalysis, I asked him why the Church remained so possessively silent on the very existence of the accumulated lore of death and communication with the dead which is the fruit of its last thousand years.

"Because," he said, "the world is not yet sufficiently scientific to deal with such knowledge." Which is very likely the case.

XV

THIS that I have been saying covers the available material that must be taken into account in arriving at a new technique of death. All of it will not be accepted but none of it can be utterly disregarded. There is also much modern knowledge, not yet coordinated into any system, most of it incidental to various sciences which have not had the nature or behavior of consciousness as an objective.

All this time there have been the most revolutionary changes in the attitude of science itself toward the nature of consciousness and its place in the universe. Since my contact with William James and acceptance of his idea of the brain as an organ of transmission, and consciousness as a force, a stream of energy, I have been thinking of it myself in terms analogous to other universal forces, or, as a still later concept permits, a substance analogous to electricity or light.

Other thinkers since William James have modified our concept of consciousness until it presents itself as immensely more than an activity going on within man, perhaps as the primary activity of the universe, the veritable stuffing of space. Wherever it came from, once having taken up its residence in the preferred combination of chemicophysical elements, consciousness has proceeded to modify its environment in a continuous scheme called evolution, until finally there was developed a mechanism by which self-consciousness became manifest.

The biologist will probably protest that this is an over-simplification of an immensely involved process. But the writer's purpose is merely to indicate that the theory of immortality here set forth is rooted in current concepts of life origins and processes, and that it ties up with much that is in everybody's mind about streams of energy, receiving and sending mechanisms, and their relation to what is known to go on in human consciousness.

Nobody now has the temerity to deny that consciousness, whatever its origin, behaves as if it proceeded out of inexhaustible reservoirs. It behaves like an independent form of energy that is capable of modifying its host and is modified in turn by the mechanism that exhibits it. It behaves as if Jesus were, on the whole, correct in assuming for it a universal source, the Father, a projection of it incarnated in the individual human being, the Son, and a natural passage—a wave length back and forth?—a Holy Spirit completing the connection between its source and the self-conscious entity. And within the human mechanism the modified self-conscious tip of the projection of the stream becomes something that may be differentiated by the term "human soul," if that term appeals to you. It behaves so much like the Father, Son, Holy Spirit and soul of orthodox religion that you will find that you can discuss it under those terms without abating a single jot of the severest scientific scholarship.

Of tentative conclusions about the nature of consciousness, entertained by the best minds, three or four can be taken into account. Consciousness, it is postulated, is One; one substance, one mode of energization. The differences we observe in its manifestations are due to differences in the mediums in which it is

discoverable.   There are first-rate minds willing to believe that consciousness is what we used
to think ether must be, the nexus of the material world.   There may be consciousness
manifesting in the cosmos, according to the
capacity of cosmic matter to be acted upon by
it.   There is possibly a chemic consciousness
active in chemic atoms, a vegetative consciousness in the growing plant.   A conversation
overheard between McDougal, the Botanist,
and McDougall, the Psychologist, points the
trend of thinking.   Said the Botanist to the
Psychologist, "Where do you think self-
consciousness might begin in the life of plants?"
Said McDougall, the Psychologist, after
consideration, "Possibly where there is accom-
modation between two tropisms."   "Then," said
McDougal, the Botanist, "there is self-consciousness in a daffodil."*

No two biologists quite agree over the appearance of self-consciousness in animal life,
but none deny consciousness of some sort in

*This would occur when the flower stalk of the daffodil
adjusts itself to the pull of gravity, drawing the heavy bud
down to the ground, and the tropism which impels the flower
to face the light.

all living forms. The tendency of consciousness to modify its host in a progressive scheme toward a type of instrumentation capable of sustaining a high degree of self-consciousness, may turn out to be the interior drive of evolution. At any rate, it is only the degree to which incarnate consciousness modifies its host, and not the fact of such modification, that is debatable.

Whatever may be finally determined about the relation of consciousness to the material in which it works, it is agreed that the probable modus is suggestion. Whether it be the suggestion received by the under portion of a vegetating plant cell washed constantly to and fro by the tides on a shallow coast, which results in the modification of that surface into roots, or the rhythmic insistence of the autosuggestionist, *Every day in every way* ... that is the method by which consciousness, eyeless and dumb, is affected. For the twin characteristic of consciousness, which can not be separated from suggestibility, is obedience.

Consciousness always works within the law of its material. Nowhere is it found working otherwise, so that something of the nature and direction of its activities can be discovered through a knowledge of the law of the particular substance worked upon. It is this quality of obedience to law which gives to the manifestations of consciousness their immense diversity.

Along with these salient traits, there is a persistent tendency toward form, the more persistent the urge, the more complex the form, the higher the type of consciousness. Apparently no failure of particular form through unsuitability either of use or environment, balks the invention of consciousness once it has discovered the host endowed with that especial physico-chemical constitution which in combination with consciousness produces life. There are biologists who think it no great matter for consciousness if even the human form fails. What will happen in that eventuality is a turning back upon the path and picking up of the next likeliest form to be modified for the manifestation of self-conscious intelligence, elephants or tigers, or still lower, less specialized forms.

There may be other traits and liabilities of

consciousness, considered as energetic in its nature, yet to be descried and described by science. Those just mentioned are fairly well understood, and all of them play on our side. For the average citizen it is enough to say that consciousness knows everything it needs to know for its own purpose; and that it forgets nothing; nothing that it has experienced. How far the human consciousness, for instance, is affected by or remembers what comes to it by way of pure intellectualization, nobody is prepared to say. What one must admit is that all these traits of consciousness are the ends of threads which we find tied together in our own life complex, the other ends of which, infinitely extended, are gathered into the hand of God. All we know here is, that by getting hold of these thread ends, we can, with intelligence, "work" them.

We have already seen that man's unargued conviction has been that consciousness is ever-living. Most modern thinkers would concede this, if by ever-livingness we mean that it is of the indestructible stuff of existence. What they hesitate over is the idea that our personal allotment of consciousness can be so worked upon by its human envelope that it retains that stamp after the envelope has decayed.

On the present showing, hasty and incomplete as it is, I think the chances are good; at least as good as the chances of the first queer creature that essayed life on dry land, independent of his ancestral home in the tidal border of the primordial sea; better than the chances of that first brave adventurer of the air. Even if there were proof positive that discarnate existence had never been achieved, I would, with the experience at hand, be willing to have a try at it, with all the dreadful possibilities of an utter loneliness of success.

One would begin to postulate such an undertaking to survive, on the irrepressible tendency to form, which is so characteristic of consciousness. Some sort of instrument, formed for emergent activities, has always accompanied its new ventures. Supposing an individualized spark, capable of existing in a supersensible body, in a complex of energies such as are generated by the physical complexes which we now inhabit, wouldn't it begin at once the evolution of a new envelope? There is not one iota of evidence, not even presumptive evidence, that consciousness can't exist in supersensible matter, in a supersensory body. Sir Oliver Lodge is willing to suppose that the human entity already possesses such an envelope, corresponding to the astral body of the Orient, temporarily shaped by the exigencies of present life. But once the torts and strains of that life are removed, the involved conscious entity becomes capable of independent existence. We've no evidence, really, that the soul which the Bantu see as a little thing, smaller than a grain of sand, can't exist as the positive charge of the energy of consciousness in a nest of ions, or whatever it is that science indicates as the primary constituent of matter.

We can not suppose that such a liberated consciousness would forget its long experience of form building, its intimate acquaintance with every sort of building material; nor its habit of obedience to the law of material. Since we are agreeing everywhere that the mode of consciousness is subjective, we would not anticipate its leaving behind the knowledge, exceeding that of the intelligence, of which consciousness appears always possessed. We must think of it, too, as retaining its suggestibility; and since it seems impossible to conceive intelligence as anything but a specially modified manifestation of consciousness, we must think of the soul as appearing at the threshold of the new life equipped with undiminished potentiality for all that was experienceable in its former intellectual life. So equipped why shouldn't the personal figment of consciousness have a fair start on another existence, no matter how differentiated from this?

In the beginning of such study, we would have to set aside for further evidence the decision as to whether the Oriental idea of a series of self-conscious reincarnation is truer than the Occidental idea of two phases of existence in the first of which the second is everlastingly conditioned. Because, as a matter of fact, they might both be true. Some souls might get through the first death-crisis, and others be obliged by their necessities to be born and to die again and again before they attain complete spiritual identity. The same thing would hold true of Hereafters. Strong souls might find their way about the other world with confidence, or at least a tolerable sense of adventure. But souls that had lived too entirely in their sensory and sensual reactions would have a hell of a time trying to get on without the sensual apparatus. And I have met a number of souls going about so nearly dead within their bodies that they should count themselves lucky if they attain to the *animula vagula blandula* of the ancients.

The stumbling block to many people, in conceiving an after-death existence, is the problem of personal identity, which is, of course, the problem of self-conscious memory. People who are willing to admit the escape of a soul, a living particle which proceeds at once to be born again into another body, boggle over the idea of a remembering soul. Much of this difficulty arises out of our habit of associating self-conscious memory with the brain. The realization that the major portion of our bodily processes are carried on by memories that have no seat in the brain, that never do arrive at self-consciousness, appears to insure further, in many minds, the probability that self-conscious memory—which is, as a matter of fact, almost the only purchase that consciousness makes by its experience of living—will be quite certainly left behind.

As a purely personal interpretation, it always seems to me that we might reasonably expect just the opposite; that self-consciousness, which, for all we can see and understand of the evolutionary objective, is precisely the single appreciable reward of that long process which would not be relinquished. If one can think of the universe as purposive, and many first-rate minds are thinking that, its purpose in man is to attain self-consciousness. Having won it, individual consciousness proceeds to shake off the first frail instrument, and escape with its dearly bought booty into a plane in which a still more perfect instrument can be evolved, and new gains in knowing that it knows, added to the soul's accomplishment.

It is also possible to think with the religionists of the Orient, of consciousness, passing itself successively through birth after birth until the whole tendency to form, to objectivity, the whole processes of desire and accomplishment have been worked out, humanism shucked off, as it were, and—the completely self-knowing consciousness being reabsorbed into the source—the Void itself becomes self-conscious. Knowing itself at last, it rests. But where all is guessing, and intelligence has not yet afforded much aid to our guess in this particular field, one can do no less than guess in accordance with one's experience. My experience is to have seen the whole process of which man is, in this world, the being to whom the most is vouchsafed of the Father, as a progression toward high individualization. My experience has been that at the furthest reach of my individual consciousness, when it achieves for a moment or two the Unitive Life, knowing itself in touch with the Universal, it knows not only the inexpressible, *but knows, never so explicitly, that it is inseparably a part of all experience past and to come.*

I can not now recall what I for one moment knew of the higher, as yet unachieved, states of group-mindedness, but I do recall that while knowing them, even in that instant, I knew their derivative relation to all that went before. And I have no doubt whatever that in the course of time mankind will arrive at experiencing those higher states, as freely as we now experience the states known as "mob" states, the states of the swarm, the herd and the pack. What I bring back from my most illuminative experiences, is the certainty that the highest states of consciousness are states of "recollection," that is to say they are states of extraordinarily high clarification of *memory,* moments in which *all* of the individual consciousness is unfolded, extended, made of one piece and one texture, that which we call past as well as that we call future.

When I speak of memory I mean something more than an alteration taking place in the gray matter shut up within a skull. I am thinking of the process by which the experience of the race, the experience of the human species, the experience of the ancestral animal species, is carried in the under-consciousness of man, to reissue as genius, as intuitive promptings called hunches, as dreams, as obscure processes of healing going on in hidden tissues, as reproduction, and as new species. No one denies that we have such memories, and no one supposes that their seat is in the brain. They are found going on in creatures that have no brains; they pass— if they pass on a bridge of body-stuff called germ plasm, and not by unguessed mechanisms of consciousness itself—from generation to generation, by particles so minute as to escape detection by man's unaided senses. And some of these submerged experiences have a way of floating up to the level of intellectual consciousness with no less of poignancy. There is, for example, the sensation experienced in sleeping dreams, and even as day-dreams, of floating, of moving freely through the air, by a mere act of volition, which psychologists tell us is a memory, a million-million-year-old memory of being carried to and fro on tides of shallow seas as ancestral entities of undifferentiated protozoa.

Sometimes these submerged memories, when they reach the threshold, fail so completely to connect with our information concerning our evolutionary experience, that they are not recognized.

Among primitives there is an experience usual enough, although it may not occur to every individual, to be generally accepted at its face value. It comes to tribal men in slightly somnolent or detached states, when one is resting after exertion, or walking along not thinking of anything in particular. Suddenly a plant, a stone, an animal, will prick itself out of the environment, will take on unrationalized connotations of importance, will seem, even, to start a little from its background, exist independently of it, and impress itself so meaningfully upon the attention that Indians say of it, "It speaks to me."

Any object, animate or inanimate, which has so impressed itself upon any person, has for him a particular significance. He thinks of it as good for his luck, his health, or likely to increase his own *wakonda,* his personal power. After I had had years of association with tribesmen I began to have this experience myself. By inquiry, I learned that cowboys, sheep-herders, and forest rangers—men whose business is much out-of-doors—had it also. But nobody could explain it.

Then one afternoon I was drifting in a glass-bottomed boat alongside one of the Channel Islands, and the boatman had let down on a string some sort of bait, to lure the finny inhabitants of the island sea-gardens within range of my observation. I saw the lovely fairy shapes glide up from under ferny weed and mottled stone, to hang quiveringly about the strange object, toward which they began to exhibit eager excitement, subtle alterations of pose, twitchings and tremors by which one clearly understood that the phenomenon called "recognition" was taking place in them. This the psychologists agree upon as perhaps the earliest motion of self-consciousness, a reaction probably involving the whole physical complex, since it occurs in creatures that have no sensory or intellectual apparatus to which it may be referred, apprizing the living entity that here is something pertinent to its well-being, something to be delightedly absorbed, made part of itself. . . . *Recognition!* Intuitive certainty of absolute rightness. Oh, ecstasy! Do we not

still admit ecstasy in the recognition of the
mate, and a kind of romantic authenticity in
our disregard of all other considerations? Is
not all our language of love touched still with
the reactions of this primary biological recognition, "I could eat you up." "I could kiss you
to death."

Leaning far over not to disturb the rapture
of little fishes, it dawned upon me that this, of
course, was what happened to me and to the
Indians when anything wordlessly "spoke" to
us. It must have been thus that creatures lately
of the sea learned what to eat on dry land;
thus that the Dawn-man learned to know not
only his proper food but herbs that were good
to be eaten for certain conditions of dis-ease:
an incredibly ancient experience rising to the
threshold of self-consciousness, as we say, "remembered." With such recognitions comes
such an emotion as the mystic feels when he
becomes aware of certainties of which his intelligence is unable to take the measure; recognition and ecstasy. But, also, this tendency of
experience to recur, under circumstances having no relation to utility, is precisely the in-

dispensable trail of genius which we call temperament; "emotion recollected in tranquillity." Without it artistic "creation" is impossible. Is it not a fair assumption that consciousness makes some such use of such recollection, that it may indeed be equally indispensable to the constitution of life after death?

I think we may at least accept it as natural that the after-death memory will partake of this subjective quality; it will be like other survival memories, directly related to those experiences which have been involved with the essential evolutionary processes. I am not sure that intellectual memories will survive at all. Identity should survive in most cases, because it is so involved with all our subjective experience; although I can easily imagine that there are persons who live so persistently in their surface reactions, who know so little of deep-life, that they might have difficulty in remembering who they are. Certainly there must be a great deal forgotten. That may be one of the reasons why, if mediumistic reports are to be accepted as evidential, so little is offered, and that little so trivial, as proof of identity.

What we remember other people by is their objectivity, their looks, manners, little habits and quirks of personality. What the discarnate would logically remember themselves by, would be their subjectivity, the hidden and, in this life, largely inarticulate experiences. We might even, those of us who have little self-knowledge here, have difficulty over there in identifying ourselves.

It is because I am awake to the possibilities of memory losses in discarnation, that I have urged my Catholic friends to make, with all the resources of the Church at hand, a publicly contributive study of the supposed after-death behavior of saints. I say "supposed" not to cast any reproach upon the belief in saints, but merely to allow for the widest range of approach to phenomena. It would be the saints, the poets and creative workers generally, all the types of humans who have a liberal subjective life, that I would expect to survive, and to retain, if anybody does, some sort of potency in this life they have left behind. And I would expect a great many of them—Francis of Assisi, for instance— to do just about what he is supposed to do when appealed to from this side. We have all become so habituated to the idea that the healings wrought by relics of dead saints are wrought by suggestion, solely through the subconscious of the applicant, that it requires a certain gymnastic of the mind to reconsider the possibility that the essential part of Francis is still making his habitual response.

Suggestion works both ways; it is not reasonable to suppose that the impression made on Francis by human misery in his time, would fail to survive with anything of him that is survivable. And in our modern time we fail to realize how recent, how very recent is this medical science that does such wonders in relieving human anguish. We forget how short a time ago sickness was a mysterious and nearly inescapable universal affliction. We can scarcely measure the response, in times past, of warm natures to the appeal of unrelievable misery; and we are bound to believe that the unmedicined pain and the anguish of impotence to help, which characterized the Middle Ages, are not without a long lasting effect on the subconscious of the race, both for the dead

and the undead. I say that it is a denial of all
that we think we have learned about the subconscious of the race, to deny that the gentle-
hearted who died in those days, might not set
in motion just such attempts at alleviation as
are credited to them. If Eugene Debs came
back, would he be, do you think, answering
silly questions of identity in the back parlors of
pseudo-intellectuals, or exercising his powers
in attempts to get across to the poor, the under-
privileged, dumb of mind and yearning of
heart, on whose behalf he spent himself while
here? If I come back, where do you think I
would be drawn by those deep currents of being
which are so much more to humanity than mind,
but here among the simple souls among whom
I have experienced so much, here, or in Mexico
where there is more need? If the evidence of
biology and ethnology and psychology mean
anything at all to us, this is what they mean,
that it is experience that survives, not necessarily the fruit of experience, but the experience itself with its increased capacity for more
experience. And if any part of the fruit of
experience survives, it would be the sense

of identity which is augmented by memories of experience, which is the chain upon which relationships between experiences are established and self-conscious evolution made possible. By memory, in this case, I mean the tendency of experience subjectively recorded, to recur, as all our science admits that it does. Whether the small change of experience that never pierces below the level of surface attention will come back after death is of no importance. A great deal of it—telephone numbers for instance—fails to recur even in life.

XVI

OF THE soul as a separable, highly individualized entity, man has imagined a great deal and learned very little. He began thinking about it as an intangible—as intangible as his breath—supersensible replica of himself, or at least if not always retaining the detailed shape of himself, capable of resuming that shape on occasion, or even of assuming the shapes of other men or animals. He thought of it as equipped with volition, all the emotions, and many of the intellectual capacities of his living self; but never exactly like himself. Among practically all tribes the dead are thought of as either diminished or augmented in their natural powers. Especially they are thought of as having a superior capacity for moving through space, and subject to a dreadful destiny of punishment or reward, of unending duration. Practically all these suppositions about the dead on examination are seen to be objectifications of those motions which consciousness seems to make of itself, motions in which it appears to act independently of time and space and the volitions of its host.

Scarcely any ancient people questioned the actuality of this nimble, invisible other self whose activities consisted largely of dreams, premonitions, clairvoyance, auditions, visions, every sort of perception of Reality unconnected with sensory apparatus. We ourselves are descended from peoples who for nearly two thousand years, have been ostensibly chiefly occupied with concern for this invisible guest and its continued existence in a world better suited to its constitution. Therefore, it is not surprising, but strikes one oddly at times to discover how, now that interest has shifted from the soul-entity to the behavior of soul-stuff, we are prevented from adequate reconcepts of souls and their constitution, by the persistence of more primitive pictures in our heads. This has been more than a little evident in the confessions of conspicuous people, so popular of late, as to what they do and do not accept concerning soul life. There has been more than a little of this sort of thing in American magazines in which the inexpertness of the man in the street is flattered by the equal inexpertness of the eminent—and this is perhaps one of the dreadful menaces which Democracy brings upon itself—who because they may have invented mathematical formulas or organized successful institutions, are supposed to become, automatically, authorities on everything else. And in practically all of these confessions of the want of faith in souls and soul life, it is the soul concepts of antiquity, concepts that are no longer accepted by genuine specialists in this field, that are, with sweeping gestures of superior intellectualization, rejected. I have seen a lot, lately, of this sort of straw-valiency of disbelief in religious concepts which, after my association with Medicine Men, Cardinals, Heads of Religious Orders, Poets, Psychologists, Biologists, Folklorists and other workers in this field, I did not know that *anybody* considered worth talking about. And the odd characteristic of so many of these rejections of early Victorian orthodoxy, is that they contain within themselves essential contradictions.

Few of these public heresies deny any of

the postulates about consciousness, or the modern reports of its behavior within its host, except the one that relates to the eventuation of an entity called a soul. It is quite possible to discover scientists who accept the mystic states, and will even admit their pertinence to scientific discovery—I am thinking of Kukelé and his dancing atoms, or of Einstein and his mystical attitude toward space—but they deny the universal conclusion of mysticism as to the soul and its continuing entity. Incontinently, many of them rest their conviction of the non-existence of the soul, on the newest evidence of the universality and constant character of the reactions between the sensible and the supersensible elements in man's make-up. Everything is admitted as to the essential nature of consciousness, its obedience, its suggestibility, its capacity for the recurrence of experience, especially that experience which antedates the brain. Not because the sensitivities of consciousness include responses to such incidents as sticking your feet out from under cover on a cold night, carrying around with you particles of undigested food, the dominant activity of one gland or another, are you supposed to be soulless. Not because along with the memory of rocking about in primordial seas, consciousness retains a memory of your youthful resentment at not being permitted to eat gooseberry tart when you had the mumps; not because of the intensity and variety and, on the whole, law-obeying multiplicity of what is modernly discovered to be going on in every one of us, is it thought logical to conclude there is nothing there at all. We are treated to a free discussion of all, even the most intimate of our "reactions," so long as we continue to profess a profound skepticism as to there being anything real and discussable that reacts.

With the flood of modern discovery as to the nature of behavior, one is likely to find oneself in need of a concept that allows for all the new items. And this necessity is most likely to be felt by people who have not yet rid themselves of the fallacy of belief. It is only recently that we have found a cosmic concept that accounts for all the stars, and we have it on the authority of the best astronomers that there are a number of items of astronomical knowledge not yet accommodated by it. This does not greatly upset us, since we have long recovered from our notion that what we believed about the stars made any difference to them or to us. But we are still more or less affected by a habit of thinking that what we believe or do not believe about the soul affects, normally *should* affect, what we do about it. We are all convinced that *if* it is demonstrated past a doubt that we have souls, we *ought* to do something about it.

I find this idea of the importance of the individual soul to itself universal and constant, and therefore to be taken into account. Such a notion occurs so early in the history of mankind that it must be intaught, something that consciousness knows about itself. It belongs with the other things consciousness knows about itself, such as that it can be increased by its own motions, that it can modify its host, that it more or less struggles with its host for control, that its modifications are largely in the direction of developing a self-knowing intelligence.

In a general way I readily accept the probability that consciousness takes up its residence in my highly individualized mechanism, with the idea of working out for itself a stable entity. I have a notion, which has not yet assumed the fixity of a belief, that the fear of death is, to a great measure, the resistance of consciousness to being deprived of its instrument for such development, before its desire of self-continuing existence has been satisfied. I have another notion that the acceptance of death may be related to other motions of consciousness, such as its failure of drive, or of realization that the present instrument has served its turn.

My deliberate avoidance of belief rests upon the observation which any biologist and many psychoanalysts will confirm, that the movement of subjective consciousness may be immeasurably slow; that separated from intelligence, consciousness is capable of remaining for ages almost static. I remember when I lived in the desert west of Death Valley, I was acquainted with figments of consciousness that had got entangled in the form of a tortoise eons ago when Death Valley was a sea-bottom, and had gone on there ever since, not having learned anything new except to subsist in a state of desertness brought by ages of slow increase to the superlative degree. Having in mind this capacity for accepting suggestion from its environment, which consciousness exhibits, I have a notion that the soul could be rendered fixed by a belief, so that it would resist even the shock of death to release it. And on the other hand, I understand that by a contrary belief, a soul, that is to say, a highly individualized consciousness, could be started on a path of unprecedented activity. I have thought for a long time that what Jesus meant when he said the Father hath delivered Judgment to the Son, is something quite different from what the phrase meant to the painter of the Sistine Chapel. I think by judgment, he meant intellectual determination, and by the son, he meant the individual projection of consciousness which is nested in man. This means to me that self-knowing intelligence is of immense importance to the development of souls, of importance to the ultimate evolution of consciousness.

I suppose that what most people mean when they demand something to "believe," is that before they can undertake spiritual activity on their own account, they have to experience intellectual determination. Consciousness, for them, is not self-starting. But for me such activity has been continuous and explorative. If I entertain no very positive conclusions about the nature of the soul and the mechanics of its escape from the body, it is because I realize that there is tremendous study going on in that department of science, of which no complete report has yet been made. In laboratories all over the world, inquiry is being made into the constitution of the soul, its relation to time and space, its entanglement with the manifestations called personality, its faculties called supernormal for no good reason except that modern life has driven them underground. Studies are going on in the reach and method of hypnotism, of hetro- and autosuggestion, and especially in that singular experience known as multiple personality. It does not seem surprising in view of the variety of the aspects of soul, that the modern who lacks the authority of the inknowing experience, would conclude that he hasn't any soul because of the difficulty of separating it from its by-products.

Among ancient peoples, the Egyptians thought most and most informedly about the complexity of the soul. For them there was not only the spirit, which was the identical individual, with a kind of soul of its own, a constituent particle of self-existing energy, which, after death, went on to the company of the gods and gradually reassembled to itself all that it required for a completely expressive existence. There was the *ka,* which remained behind "haunting" the tomb, the mummy, the personal property of the dead. There was the *ba,* which took up its residence in other men, undoubtedly the intellectual projection of the phenomenon known as "possession" or of multiple personality. There were other items of soul, but these in particular indicate that all the soul complexities that trouble modern men were experienced by the Egyptians. There are still reliable alienists who lean to a belief of possession. I am inclined myself to see in the world-wide and ancient tales of hauntings, as well as in the modern phenomena of psychometry, and certain of the phenomena of mediumship such as "materializations," a possibility that there might be a *ka,* a pseudo-soul, a personality ghost, sloughed off in death, carrying with it certain marks of identity, haunting the familiar places and properties of the dead, dropping at last like the spent corolla of the flower of personality—of which the soul is the seed. In our introspective moments we are all aware of these enfoliated layers of selves, of secondary personalities overridden by the central drive, of shadow selves in which, under certain conditions, we temporarily exist. The possibility of a lingering survival of some of these may yet have to be taken into account.

Of the constitution of the immortal, separable soul not much can be predicated. It will possess consciousness, of course, enmeshed in whatever medium is necessary to the existence of consciousness in individual shape. Somehow it isn't possible for us to imagine consciousness without some sort of medium as a nucleus upon which to erect an instrument, which in our experience of consciousness is native to it. Nor can we think of consciousness stripped of any of the characteristics with which we are familiar, knowingness, suggestibility, obedience, and the capacity for reexperiencing its essential motions, which is the sort of memorability upon which identity could be predicated.   Nor is it easy to conceive consciousness as robbed by death of self-knowing intelligence, such intelligence as has been genetically related to its experience.   I am doubtful about the survival of a great many of the intellectual tricks, such as characterize mind at various periods; more doubtful still of the carrying over of mere information acquired in this life and never experientially utilized.

And finally, I do not see how we can escape carrying over the impetus given to the released consciousness, through its susceptibility to suggestion, by our habitual spiritual attitudes, our deeply rutted thinking about death and the soul's destiny.

This is the utmost I can draw from the material of my life, to inform the occasion of my death.   Except that I fear I have not clearly conveyed a conclusion which is the whole conceptual basis of my thought on these matters. It is that the *felt experience* of life must, in any conclusion of mine, always take precedence of the orthodoxies of science. The problems of life and death are largely subjective problems. I can admit science as a method which has an explicit, but not predominant, applicability to subjective experience. Science may explain, but I do not permit the experience to be confined within or constrained by the method.

I make this rule for myself out of a profound experience of my own that the *method* of consciousness, or God, if you will, is not the method of the scientist, but of the creative artist.

I hesitate here, having in mind my own warning against attempting to explain intellectually what is subjectively apprehended. The Creative Factor in the universe does not work like a scientist who knows nothing and has it all to prove and find out, but like a novelist who knows it all, and strives only to arrange what he knows in patterns that will best display its attributes, its inwardness, its truth. Even the patterns which consciousness makes with its living material, the new species patterns out of new combinations of unit factors, seem to be made by the same law of inherent possibility that governs the combinations taking place in the subconsciousness of the novelist. Out of three or four carefully observed types of hero, brooded upon, suddenly I wake to find a new character, the more living as he is the more completely assembled without my conscious attention. Underneath all creativeness of worlds and works of art, there are necessities, which the scientist calls laws, and the artist, plot or composition, essential designs. The business of the scientist is to penetrate and to divide all objectivity and search out the pattern thereof, which is the law of its constitution. It is the business of the artist to feel—to apprehend subjectively—the underlying plot or pattern upon which he builds something that displays its meaning. What every artist knows is, that in respect to the material worked upon, he is using precisely the same laws as the scientist. What all but a few of the greatest scientists refuse to admit, is that the process of assembling the laws and materials of subjectivity, is the artist process. Biologists seem to agree upon the mechanism of species formation, but the law eludes precise definition. Unable for the most part properly to evaluate *works of art,* the lesser sort of scientists tend to discredit the processes by which they are made to take place. Because the scientist, in his devotion to pure intellectualization, is obliged to inhibit in himself elements which are indispensable to the artist, he often automatically inhibits himself from realizing the clean hard integrity of devotion to law which underlies all great works of art as well as of science. He fails to understand that the loyalty of the artist is owed to his *experience* of truth rather than to his rationalization of it. It is very difficult to make a scientist admit that you can have an experience of law without a rationalization of it. And by cutting himself out of the artist process, such a scientist remains still outside the essential process of creation.

I have said that, as a girl, I had a disposition toward mathematics a little beyond what was thought proper to girls, but that I had absolutely no talent for it. This means exactly what it means when one is moved by music and can not produce it. Later I discovered a recurrent appetite for mathematical refreshment, which was satisfied by reading anything in that line that was just a trifle beyond my capacity to deal with intellectually. I read anything that brought me up on the tiptoes of my mind, and found all my creative processes augmented, raised to higher levels. I hadn't thought very much why this should be the case, simply filed away the information for use in periods of dryness and loss of creative power. When a story didn't "go," I took down my geometry, as a last resort, and had a bout with it. Then, one day I got into a Fifth Avenue bus and sat down in front of two men who were avidly discussing a lecture they had just heard on the mathematics of proportion as applied to art, to Greek vases in particular. I drank it in; I knew my stuff when I heard it. Fortunately the talkers went all the way to the Metropolitan Museum— I forgot what I had started out to do—and I stuck to them, eavesdropping shamelessly until they left the bus, and I with them, demanding to know where I could hear more and

from whom. It was, the subject of their discussion, as you may have guessed, Hambidge's
Dynamic Symmetry. Afterward I bought the
book, took it to the woods with me and made
it part of my experience. For those who do
not know the work in question, it may be described as a careful exposition of the mathematics of growth, a knowledge of which—but
whether felt or apprehended no one really
knows—underlies all Greek art; recovered and
made modernly intelligible by J. Hambidge.
It is not very abstruse, but I should not like,
many times as I have been through the book,
to be called upon to demonstrate without re-
viewing it. I couldn't, in fact, solve the equa-
tion which Sinclair Lewis postulates as
marking the turning point at which *Arrow-
smith* left off being a medical man, and began
to be a scientist, though I might have when I
left College. I can't read Einstein, of course,
but I do read Bertrand Russell and others who
interpret him, and this is what happens to me.
I read on in a sort of intellectual trance, similar
to the trance of music, not remembering what
I read, possibly not apprehending it. . . . I

should say that the meaning goes past me as great music goes, as the splendor of a sunset. And afterward, I find pictures and patterns in my mind that I recognize vaguely as being derived from my mathematical reading. I am aware of the underlying structure of my own work firming to principles felt to be universal rather than personal. I find my unpremeditated ideas of space and time becoming more fluent; my apprehension of reality more dynamic. Something in me knows more mathematics, makes better use if it, than I do.

I am acquainted with business men and engineers who say they get similar clarifications by listening to good music of which they know no more than I do of synthetic tensors. But music helps me not at all except pleasurably, the emotional overtones and inclusions soothe rather than excite subconscious activity. If I were to write under the influence of the sonata Eroica, I might get the composer's pattern but not an original, fundamental structure of human behavior, such as is primarily a behavior of consciousness. But I can get subjectively at such structures by reading mathematics beyond my capacity intellectually to understand.

And that is why I say that the challenge is from the artist and the mystic to the scientist. There is undoubtedly a mathematical structure that will explain the alteration in consciousness involved in the experience called death; but it is as experience that death changes must first be met and resolved. And I think the joke is on Mr. Einstein and Mr. Russell if, in saying that I meet death as an artist, I nevertheless can say that I meet it in better countenance for what I have been able to get out of a less—or more than—intellectual consciousness of mathematics. I get it as a poet gets a poem, or a painter a picture, out of knowledge pushed down below the threshold, refused until it has been lost completely and then recovered by the intelligence. Every creative artist knows exactly what I mean by the law that must be forgotten before it will work fruitfully.

If death is a gate, and not the dead end of the passage, I shall get through by means of what I have learned as folklorist, as mystic, as artist. But, except by a direct revelation from the other world, which, without expecting it, one admits as possible, I am convinced we shall not be able to rationalize immortality without the help of the highest type of scientific intelligence. All the activities of life, and not only human life but all those in which consciousness is evident or can by any manner of means be descried as playing a part; and all the departments of such activity, not only those called intellectual, but the creative, the mystical, the activities of genius, of protective mimicry, of the so-called artistic temperament as well as the religious temperament, all the activities within the shadow of which stands God, must be scrutinized, identified, set in order. Then perhaps we shall produce a satisfactory philosophy of the soul. And in the meantime the artist and the mystic will know what they know.

XVII

To MOST people the problem of survival is a question of what they personally shall do about it. People who are no longer able to be satisfied with the orthodox explanations of the spiritual life, and are still convinced of the reality of that life, are greatly concerned to know, since it is not a psalm-singing Heaven they are to live for, what after-death conditioning, what contingencies they are to prepare to meet. Among primitives, and even among us, there is often an instinctive trust in the event, probably not unlike the prompting a bird has of the rightness of migration, an impulse to go away from here, and a complete coordination of every other impulse with it. But when death is far from us, and life over-full of complexities, for which no inexorable event calls the turn, when we are unable to feel certain what we do live for, it is natural to question the end, natural to look forward to death as at least one certainty about which there is no question except the inevitable question: What next?

There is no doubt that to most people a rational certainty about the life-to-come, would be welcome as providing a resolution of present difficulties. This is the most usual argument which people make to themselves, that there *must* be a focal point at death, since life, as we know it, seems so utterly without plan or direction.

Suppose then such study as I have indicated could be made, suppose every issue of life could be skilfully interrogated, every intimation gathered up into what could be accepted as a determining concept of immortality. Suppose we were, on the whole, unable to reject the evidence that life is ever-living, and that, whether or no, we must all partake of it. What would that do to our *way* of life, to our morals, to our social constitution and our spiritual behaviors?

Unless the revelation of the fact of survival were accompanied by considerable detail as to the mode of immortality, the geography of the Hereafter, the probable progressions of life there, it would make less difference than most people suppose. Man has always lived instinctively as though life were indestructible and the soul his most precious part. There has never been a time, and scarcely any people among whom the idea of making "a good end" has not been associated with a good life hereafter. To the people of to-day who have either acquired spiritual poise or complete spiritual insensibility, the announcement of irrefutable proof of survival, without any details, would make no difference at all. Other people who are at present in a muddle of incertitudes, would be driven back into the religion which seems to them to present the most rational concept of Hereafter, and there would be a swift reaction into other-worldliness among them, such as prevailed in Europe five hundred years ago.

But suppose that a general reversion to a belief in immortality carried with it much of what seems to the writer intimated. Suppose the certainty of survival put us in the way of further exploration of the Hereafter by the scientific method, further assurance of eventualities that would have to be met. Then we could look for an immediate revision of all our methods of education. Once it is understood that subjectivity is of equal if not greater importance than intellectualization in a life cycle clearly accepted as evolutionary throughout its whole extension, the entire treatment of these matters would be changed.

This would please the really great educators, most of whom have some such notion at the present time. It would put an end to the purely ritualistic aspects of education, the stuffing of young minds with assorted odds and ends of information, the emphasis on objective rather than subjective experience. School curricula would have to include, along with arithmetic, history and physics, the arts of recollection, meditation, and post-graduate courses in prayer and the Unitive Life.

The change in our morals would be of infinite relief. Few people really want to be immoral —which means being committed to behaviors that are generally believed to make against rather than for a happy and successful life. Much of current immorality arises in frank skepticism of the current criteria of morals, or affirmative declarations of belief in just the opposite. But a morality which could be confidently referred to scientific deductions from verifiable data would give a new sense of adventure to the personal life, a sense which it has, for some time now, gone limpingly without. It would rid us from the incubus of disappointed parental expectation. Since alterations in moral values would not only be expected with each new orientation of the soul toward the future, these would be considered creditable to achieve.

As for changes in religiosity which would occur with such an enlargement of our view of the Hereafter, in the direction indicated, these would be personal rather than institutional. There would be the same, possibly an increased need for priests and ministers of grace, for offices of instruction and consolation. There would certainly be an intensified interest in, and use of, ritual and ritualized prayers, since ritual is, so far, the best discoverable method of affecting the subconscious to habitual motions. And if prayer is to be scientific, the untrained mind can scarcely trust its own spontaneous gestures for anything so important. It is not postulated that a scientific verification of immortality will necessarily and inevitably make any pronounced difference in our concept of God, only in our approach to whatever we call by that name.

It seems never to have occurred to those who foresee the successful issue of what is called "psychic research," that we will not be any the less under the necessity of myth-making to express those aspects of Immaterial Reality that elude our still finite and intellectually limited conceptual faculties. Just as Jesus, who is the most modern of the prophets, was driven to the use of parables and figurative analogies *(The Kingdom of Heaven is like unto———),* so the prophets of science are constrained to the myth of mathematics, intelligible only to each other, to express the otherwise inexpressible. But even as the tribesmen saw the Sun, the Moon, and Stars as gods walking, Rain and Cloud and Thunder, people of the middle Heaven, so the man in the street to-day must see $\frac{1}{ab-x}$, $\sqrt{ab}$, y^n, indexing the mysteries of the Universe, as Blessed Personages, Angels and Archangels, choiring about their Lord. Some sort of explicit figure in the mind seems necessary to our thinking. Individual man must walk by the light he has. He must be free to use the speech that is the choice of his soul.

Not in anything discoverable about the nature of the soul, nor in the mind of any major prophet of the soul, is there ground for assuming that at the single stroke of death, everything is achieved that is within the possibility of consciousness. Even though one rose from the dead in response to the Researches, after the first shock of excited surprise, it is not at all likely that any greater alteration would take place in our attitude toward Immaterial Reality, than would be the case if science should confidently announce that life could be generally prolonged for a thousand years. It is not possible to think of immortality as a miracle, performed on behalf of men. It is an inherent possession—or it isn't. Consciousness either survives the death of the body or dies with it. If it survives, it must be in possession of all its inherencies, unaltered save for those incidental variations owed to the nature of its physical host.

We can not, therefore, suppose that death

is the end of any adventure except that of
the body. Jesus taught that it is the end of the
adventure of reproduction *(neither marriage
nor giving in marriage)*, the end of disease and
bodily pain. But no one has ever taught that
it is the end of those casualties to which individual consciousness has been more or less liable
throughout its long history on the earth. We
must go slowly here, more slowly even than
science has gone about separating the disorders
of consciousness which are developed apparently within itself, and those occasioned by the
faulty constitution or decay of the instrument.
Modern pathology seems to have arrived definitely at the point of accepting unhappy individual states of consciousness as susceptible
of being worked upon directly, without any
reference to physical ailments, a conclusion
widely entertained by tribal man. By means of
hypnotism, suggestion, prayer, psychoanalysis,
by purposive relations of a healthy consciousness to consciousness out of joint with itself,*
modern therapy does seem to be able to bring

---

* Mental healing is perhaps the best term for what I have
in mind: the direct power of mind over mind, as distinguished
from faith healing, which implies the operation of belief.

positive relief to disorganized souls. It is, of course, possible that, in leaving the body behind, we rid ourselves of the liability to such disorder, but by no means certain. No rational view of life after death would be justified in neglecting the possibility that there will be like disorders in the discarnate soul, no matter how enveloped.

Long observation of and meditation upon the behaviors of consciousness in lower life-forms, convince me that many so-called "pathological" behaviors of human beings are resurgent behaviors that were "normal" in the life-levels in which they occurred. They are only "abnormal" in intelligent beings, because no longer necessary, no longer related to the needs of the species. A single illustration will have to serve although many others may be found scattered through my other works, noted because of interest or curiosity, or in the works of any other naturalist. That same Death Valley tortoise whose ancestral line had survived an incredible evolution through conditions pointing the furthest possible reach away from his ancestral home, had a trick of preserving himself through the winter by burrowing deep in the sand, letting go his conscious life and his intelligence, which for his family was acute, for three months or so, after which he emerged in a condition that indicated an augmented vitality. He proceeded at once to reproduce his kind, and renew his growth. Among other creatures, the process of gestation actually goes on during the seasonal recession of consciousness. The point is that there is such a recession of consciousness, and that it is normal for their kind.

Modern psychology discovers such recessions in man, not always accompanied by physical apathy; infantile regressions, prenatal regressions, made in the face of swift or unwelcome demands on the energies of consciousness. These, and many other behaviors of consciousness such as the "playing possum" trick, reproduced among humans as trance or various so-called "hysterical" manifestations, are in my mind as natural to men as to other animals, except that among humans we expect them to be inhibited by intelligence. Being natural, they are possibly behaviors that might recur under the shock of death. Especially they might recur if death were met, as we read it often was met in the days when Hell was an explicit menace to the dying, with almost insane fright. And that brings us around to what was said earlier about the death song, the death rite as a self-preservative gesture of the psyche.

What I am trying to get at is the necessity, if we are to get at any rightness of the knowledge of death, of shucking off this modern obsession of "normal" and "abnormal." The normal way of triumphing over death may lie in some of the behaviors that proved so useful long before the human complex was invented. My desert tortoise, whose name was Pilot—he was born near Pilot Knob—was not a psychopath. He learned to know his name, and to prefer fresh lettuce and bread softened in milk, to desert shrubs, and to distinguish my step from that of a casual stranger. He never forgot how to take care of himself in winter; and I lost him at last, one season when he had to go so far in search of a mate that he never came back. How do you know that the very longing for everlasting sleep, in your willingness to let go the whole achievement of self-consciousness for the sleep of death, is not the evidence of a necessary cesura, in which you gather the energy of ever-livingness for a new lease of life? One thing I am sure of, if sleep is what you want, rest from the excited whirl of modern personal complexities, there is no reason why you shouldn't have it. Perhaps your remote ancestors rehearsed the trick for you against just this emergency.

With me it will not be so. The habit of life which I have cultivated is such that I can seldom sleep comfortably in my bed unless I give that other one in me something to work on, a problem to resolve, a story to work out, a mass of miscellaneous information to assort. Once the other half of me is suitably occupied, I sleep the allotted hours, and wake refreshed, with an appetite for what I have to do. It will probably be so when I die, that I will be up and about in the shortest possible interval. Very likely I shall be one of those who, according to world-old stories, do not discover for some time that they are dead.

For the people who have had so much of success in this life that they would not be without it in the next, or so little that they can't bear the idea of not having a better turn, there is much that can be done, even in the limited state of our knowledge of ourselves, with a reasonable expectation of profit. The expectation, of course, is based upon the inherited behaviors of consciousness, and its characteristic suggestibility.* What we suggest to an ever-living entity, before the event, will be remembered.

It would seem unwise to think much about personal death beforehand, especially not to think explicitly of its mode and the manner of life hereafter. It might turn out to be something quite different, so that the neophyte might be left in the condition of those unhappy humans who imagine life too explicitly in adolescence, and spend the rest of their term complaining because it isn't at all like that. It would be worse than unwise to think fearfully

* It is also possible that we shall have the help of our friends. Curiously enough, there isn't in the whole field of folklore the least stiver of evidence that it ever entered man's mind that he wouldn't join his friends after death. Even Hell is always presented as well populated; it was left for man, rather than devils, to imagine solitary confinement.

of death, or to get such a Heaven and Hell fixation as the Christian world had a few hundred years ago. Probably the fear of death— as distinguished from the fear of dying, which is a normal self-preservative reaction—is a Christian heritage. Mexico is the only country I know where death, aside from its implications of personal grief, is treated humorously, where children are given candy skulls and toy hearses to play with.

The ancient Egyptians had formulas for those who suffered the fear of death to a disturbing degree, excellently devised to act suggestively . . . and it is still open to man to make himself a death song, or adopt any form of words that will see him through more comfortably. . . . *(I am Osiris and rest in him;* let me pass through the gate.)*

The consciousness of having made a suitable disposition of one's affairs is an excellent antidote to excited apprehension, and so is the performance of any death rite to which your particular frame of belief admits you. But the best of all preparations for shuffling off this mortal

* Meaning: I have identified myself with the ever-living principle.

coil, is, in view of the nature of the evidence, to have acquired fluency in the natural inter-action of subliminal consciousness and intelli-gence consciousness.

I perceive here that I have not said enough about the experience of prayer, the one spiri-tual exercise which is and has always been open to the humblest intelligence, the least flexible subconsciousness to use. Even in its least-evolved form as inarticulate but emotionally directed desire, prayer is not without effect. Made articulate, directed by the intelligence and gradually involving the whole range of consciousness, prayer becomes an incalculable power, whether measured by its effect on the user, or by its objective accomplishment. The average person, wholly uninstructed, begins usually with the emotionally driven petition: Lord, give! . . . give! . . . and keeps on until a new emotional equilibrium is reached, in the midst of which intellectual decision becomes possible. Most Protestant prayer stops there. If one goes on without instruction, one comes to a phase in which there is an answering *start* of consciousness. Intimations of the desired answer seem to arise on every side but do not eventuate. Most people who reach this stage, end by being disappointed, think of themselves as self-deluded, react from prayer in pronounced motions of disgust. In describing this phenomena to myself I have used the term "mimicry" because it seems to me to be most akin to the thing that happens in protective mimicry of nature. Think of a bird, desiring a fat insect, hoping it is not a twig, deciding to chance it. The insect, made aware by that strange something in the lesser forms of life which is not intellect but is acted upon, the bird's mingled hope and doubt, assumes the appearance of a twig by an unpremeditated reaction, which by many repetitions becomes fixed in a habit of protective mimicry.

I have checked this over too many times not to feel certain of the mechanisms involved and since have learned that W. H. Hudson, whose opportunities for observing nature untainted were so much greater than mine, was of the same opinion. It was, for me, the first step in arriving at a fairly competent solution of the mystery of prayer being answered, as, if the practitioner will persist through the incident of protective mimicry to the next stage, he will discover it invariably is. From this on, there is an orderly progression of states, touching one step and then another of a winding stair, the end of which is never reached. How far you go in that practise depends, no doubt, upon your natural spiritual endowment and your persistence. But the unanticipated, the absolute, advantage in taking the first three steps is that, with each succeeding step, the necessary fluency between the two halves of man's mind, the intelligence and the subliminal, is augmented.

This is the best way I know to acquire that complete coordination, that wholeness which is indispensable to spiritual poise. The genius way, if you have ever so little genius, is almost equally profitable, unless you are one of those who have utilized your genius for purposes that have nothing to do with spirituality. The Mystic Way, if you have the courage to walk in it intelligently, not merely for the sake of enjoying mystical emotion, not, absolutely *not* as an escape from Here and Now, results naturally in establishing a superior control over the interactions of the immediate and the subliminal centers.

All these would seem to be serviceable to the self in an emergency—such as being thrust suddenly into the Hereafter—in which the submerged consciousness is likely to be forced sharply to the lead.

It was not until I sat down to record in outline, at least, all that I have experienced which might have any bearing on the occasion in which I most needed it, that it struck me as singular that in all my explorations of the field of the unconscious, I had never yet come upon the country of the dead. I have lost those dear to me, and have had the experiences so convincing to many, warnings of the time of death, the feeling of renewed intimacy, the sense of unseen presences. I could get messages, too, for you. If you came to me full of anguished desire for communication, and I sat down with you in a mood of sympathy, I could get comforting and convincing things. But I would not know that they did not come by the same way that a new character for my novel comes when I need it, or a character, already created, suddenly takes the story in charge and interjects behaviors and incidents undreamed of by the author. Things like that happen to every creative writer. I may say, indeed, that I do know that the same mechanisms come into play, and that I am convinced that they play all along the history of consciousness as protective mimicry, as dream, as vision; making a tender story of Virgin birth out of man's unrationalized inheritance of divinity, a sacred story of kings and sheep-herders out of a revelation of the inalienable character of that inheritance for all men, whatever their degree.

What has come to me as I write, is the profound, the flooding sense of the reality and intimacy of that inheritance. It is ours, we are its offspring, it wells up in us, urges and oppresses, fills and over-fills, yearning toward complete expression as the parent yearns for expression in the child. It works in us, and we work on it. I have little to offer as argument, but in my association with tribal man it comes to me more and more convincingly that the quality of consciousness with which *we* work, is, though in some respects more informed, less liberated than that with which the Dawn-man worked. We have a price to pay for the purchase of intelligence, but the tool is worth the money. I do not find the Country of the Dead, but I come, as it were, upon the trail of the ancestors, what they, by experiencing it, put back into the sum of available consciousness. I understand now why, when I was first fearfully facing the possibility of a last illness, I wished that I had done more impulsive, more exploratory things. Because I take even my sins experiencingly, and in the emergency of possible discarnation, it is only experience that counts. "Not the fruit of experience, but experience." Not until now have I understood the insistence of so wise a psychologist as Jesus, that there is more joy in Heaven over one sinner that repents than ninety and nine that go not astray. Almost anybody repents a sin the moment he begins really to experience it as sin, the moment that he realizes that sin is usually the avoidance of some other experience which goes deeper, makes more demanding calls on consciousness. Experiencing sin as an evasion of reality, the Son becomes of more value to the Father. I hope, I hope with all my heart, that at the last I shan't be found to have been "good" (whenever in the ordinary acceptance of the term I could be called good) because it was the easier way.

It seems likely now that I shall have from a half-score to a score more years as I am, and I am consoled of my secret apprehension of coming to the end of adventures. I am quite certain now that if there is anything that snatches us from dissolution, it does not want pale ghosts that gibber in the dark. Nor yet rapt souls that stand for ever in ecstasy over a distant gleam, a spark. There will be things yet to be done, and the stuff that we work in will be the utterly familiar and still mysterious and exciting stuff of ourselves.

THE END

THE LITERATURE OF DEATH AND DYING

Abrahamsson, Hans. **The Origin of Death:** Studies in African Mythology. 1951

Alden, Timothy. **A Collection of American Epitaphs and Inscriptions with Occasional Notes.** Five vols. in two. 1814

Austin, Mary. **Experiences Facing Death.** 1931

Bacon, Francis. **The Historie of Life and Death with Observations Naturall and Experimentall for the Prolongation of Life.** 1638

Barth, Karl. **The Resurrection of the Dead.** 1933

Bataille, Georges. **Death and Sensuality:** A Study of Eroticism and the Taboo. 1962

Bichat, [Marie François] Xavier. **Physiological Researches on Life and Death.** 1827

Browne, Thomas. **Hydriotaphia.** 1927

Carrington, Hereward. **Death:** Its Causes and Phenomena with Special Reference to Immortality. 1921

Comper, Frances M. M., editor. **The Book of the Craft of Dying and Other Early English Tracts Concerning Death.** 1917

Death and the Visual Arts. 1976

Death as a Speculative Theme in Religious, Scientific, and Social Thought. 1976

Donne, John. **Biathanatos.** 1930

Farber, Maurice L. **Theory of Suicide.** 1968

Fechner, Gustav Theodor. **The Little Book of Life After Death.** 1904

Frazer, James George. **The Fear of the Dead in Primitive Religion.** Three vols. in one. 1933/1934/1936

Fulton, Robert. **A Bibliography on Death, Grief and Bereavement:** 1845-1975. 1976

Gorer, Geoffrey. **Death, Grief, and Mourning.** 1965

Gruman, Gerald J. **A History of Ideas About the Prolongation of Life.** 1966

Henry, Andrew F. and James F. Short, Jr. **Suicide and Homicide.** 1954

Howells, W[illiam] D[ean], et al. **In After Days;** Thoughts on the Future Life. 1910

Irion, Paul E. **The Funeral:** Vestige or Value? 1966

Landsberg, Paul-Louis. **The Experience of Death:** The Moral Problem of Suicide. 1953

Maeterlinck, Maurice. **Before the Great Silence.** 1937

Maeterlinck, Maurice. **Death.** 1912

Metchnikoff, Élie. **The Nature of Man:** Studies in Optimistic Philosophy. 1910

Metchnikoff, Élie. **The Prolongation of Life:** Optimistic Studies. 1908

Munk, William. **Euthanasia.** 1887

Osler, William. **Science and Immortality.** 1904

Return to Life: Two Imaginings of the Lazarus Theme. 1976

Stephens, C[harles] A[sbury]. **Natural Salvation:** The Message of Science. 1905

Sulzberger, Cyrus. **My Brother Death.** 1961

Taylor, Jeremy. **The Rule and Exercises of Holy Dying.** 1819

Walker, G[eorge] A[lfred]. **Gatherings from Graveyards.** 1839

Warthin, Aldred Scott. **The Physician of the Dance of Death.** 1931

Whiter, Walter. **Dissertation on the Disorder of Death.** 1819

Whyte, Florence. **The Dance of Death in Spain and Catalonia.** 1931

Wolfenstein, Martha. **Disaster:** A Psychological Essay. 1957

Worcester, Alfred. **The Care of the Aged, the Dying, and the Dead.** 1950

Zandee, J[an]. **Death as an Enemy According to Ancient Egyptian Conceptions.** 1960